ENDORSEMENTS

Never has there been more urgency in our land for a God-given awakening to Christ. David Bryant's vision of Christ, and the full extent of His supremacy, can bring the body of Christ together in powerfully transforming ways. We believe his message…
(is) exactly what's needed at this critical moment in America.

—from An Open Letter to the Church from 70 National Leaders (see www.ProclaimHope.com)

David Bryant has, in my estimation, the clearest and most profound Christology of any American theologian alive today. His book is a watershed treatise of what it means to have both a view of Christ and experience of Christ necessary to exercise consequential leadership in our generation.

—Dr. Mac Pier, President, The NYC Leadership Center

David Bryant has taught me a great deal but nothing as vital as the content of *CHRIST IS ALL!* Unless we restore Christ's supremacy inside the church, we will never have a message or mission for those outside the church. We keep looking for a program or technique to guide us, but here is the real answer for what we truly need to find our way home—the recovery of Christ alone, the one who has all authority in heaven and on earth!

—Dr. John Armstrong, President, ACT 3

In moments of revelation and breathtaking insight, church leaders from all backgrounds are awakening to the majesty and incomparable singularity of Christ: He is not our religion; He is our king. He is not merely our moral code; He is our unfathomable Creator. This book is one of the most riveting, captivating reads I've known. Here is a trumpet summoning the church to lift our eyes to the unparalleled splendor of our Redeemer.

—Rev. Francis Frangipane, President, Advancing Church Ministries Association

Warning! This book will surely be hazardous to your life as you have lived it,...and that's a good thing. Until *CHRIST IS ALL!* most of us did not realize how much our Lord and Savior Jesus Christ has been diminished in our Christian literature, preaching, and communal life. It will open your eyes, ears, spirit, and heart for all that Christ is.

—Roland Hinz, President, Hi-Torque Publications / Christian Radio Broadcaster

More than anyone else I know, David Bryant has a passion for Christ and a passion for a Christ Awakening throughout America and, for that matter, the whole world. This book is a distillation of what David lives and breathes so passionately, namely the exaltation of Christ among the nations. The church needs to hear this clear call so that she can march forward with a confidence that is worthy of our triumphant Savior. Read this book in the quietness of your room and then spread its message from the mountaintops.

—Dr. Erwin W. Lutzer, Senior Pastor, The Moody Church, Chicago

Next to the Bible itself, *CHRIST IS ALL!* is the most transforming Christology text I have ever encountered. My appreciation for the supremacy of God's Son has taken a quantum leap.

—Rev. Gary Frost, President, Concerts of Prayer Greater New York

CHRIST IS ALL! will capture your mind and heart and inspire your worship and obedience to Jesus Christ "for all He is." It is a clarion call that will strengthen your faith and your joy in faithfulness to Christ.

—Dr. Jerry R. Kirk, Founder, National Coalition for the Protection of Children & Families

After all we know of Jesus Christ and what He has done for us, you'd think we would all live in joyful submission to Him. But we know that is not the case. *CHRIST IS ALL!* has brought us a clear and compelling view of our Savior that can enliven our relationship with Him and, when shared with others, can powerfully unite the body of Christ in worshipping and serving Him. This new resource makes it even more understandable and usable. Please seriously consider it.

—Paul Fleischmann, President, National Network of Youth Ministries

The author of Hebrews reminds us that Jesus is "the centerpiece of everything" (Heb. 3:1, *The Message*). David Bryant's *CHRIST IS ALL!* is the most definitive book next to the Bible itself ever written to substantiate this claim.

—Dr. Dick Eastman, International President, Every Home for Christ

As a businessman, I've come to appreciate the power of focus, clarity, and simplicity. David's first book *CHRIST IS ALL!* is consummately focused as it delves deeply into apostle Paul's powerful Colossians declaration. Now the new revised version advances the same great truths with crystal clarity and profound simplicity. Don't miss the great gift this new and more accessible work is to every serious believer!

—John D. Beckett, Chairman, The Beckett Companies / Author: Loving Monday; Mastering Monday

When the church fully understands the beauty, humility, and grandeur of Jesus Christ, it will bow down to the Father in gratitude and reverence. As a man fully devoted to the proclamation of the gospel throughout the world, David Bryant adorns the doctrine of Christ in *CHRIST IS ALL!* in such a way as to give the reader a taste of the glory of God.

—Rev. Matthew W. Bennett, Founder and President, The Christian Union

My faith soars when I contemplate David Bryant's scriptural review of the glory and supremacy of Christ. My heart is sobered when I consider his message of how we have strayed from our true calling in Jesus. My vision is stretched when I challenge myself with his practical solutions. I believe this book has prophetically touched the heart of the Church's greatest need today.

—Don Peter, Associate Professor of Electrical Engineering, Seattle Pacific University

I have had the privilege to receive seven years of good theological training, but the best Christology I've heard comes from David Bryant. This is one reason I am so excited to endorse the new edition of *CHRIST IS ALL!* Oh, how we need to be saturated in the wonder of Jesus Christ! May the Lord use this smaller version to bring this vital message to a larger portion of the body of Christ.

—Rev. Dennis Fuqua, Executive Director, International Renewal Ministries, Author: Living Prayer

A Latin American theologian wrote that "hope is hearing the music of the future; faith is to dance to it." By that reckoning, David Bryant's stirring and timely book will set your toes to tapping and your heart beating faster as you pray for Christ's kingdom to come. The church needs to hear this message of hope in Christ as never before.

—Dr. Ben Patterson, Campus Pastor, Westmont College, Santa Barbara, California

David Bryant's *CHRIST IS ALL!* is a refreshing reminder and prophetic advocacy that Christ is the only answer! Unless we thirst after our Redeemer and seek to grow to His likeness, we will always be the slaves of our culture and find ourselves tossed around by current thoughts and philosophies. This new revised edition of David's work makes it highly readable yet remains faithful to the original version.

—Rev. Wilson Chang, Pastor, Rutgers Community Christian Church, New Jersey

THE NEW REVISED VERSION

CHRIST Is All!

David Bryant

CONDENSED AND UPDATED WITH

Richard Ross

Join in the Joyful Awakening
to the Supremacy of God's Son

NEW
PROVIDENCE
PUBLISHERS

Published by
New Providence Publishers Inc.
P O Box 770
New Providence, NJ 07974-0770

Design and Layout
Sahlman Art Studio Inc.
20515 Rio Oro Drive
Cornelius, NC 28031

Library of Congress Catalog Number: 2010912240
International Standard Book Number (ISBN) 978-0-9755038-2-9
Printed in the United States of America

Table of Contents

A Personal Word from David Bryant

From Manifesto to Movement

This book is not a rehash of old Sunday school lessons on the life of Jesus. Quite the opposite. *CHRIST IS ALL! (CIA)* opens a new point of departure for your walk with God's Son. It explores nothing less than the full scope of His supremacy. It does so in anticipation of, and preparation for, something almost too wonderful to hope: a fresh work of God's Spirit among God's people to enlarge our vision of the reigning majesty of God's Son. The promise is poised ... impending ... bearing down upon us. It is a God-given Christ Awakening, meant for the whole Church, in every part.

Awake! Adore! Arise!

Several years ago Richard and I had the privilege of serving with a team of national youth ministry leaders to facilitate an event called PARADISE. This first-of-its-kind national youth worship gathering assembled 3,000 teenagers and adults from nearly 30 states coast to coast one warm May morning on a farm field near the center of the nation. For nearly seven hours, with absolutely no visible human leadership, we stood before a gigantic homemade throne to offer up songs, Scriptures, and prayers. These high school and college young people focused an entire day exclusively on Christ's supremacy. PARADISE was divided into three segments: Awake! Adore! Arise!

That's because *every* fresh, Spirit-infused revelation of Christ's glory follows this same threefold pattern: First, Christians wake up to more of Christ and His Kingdom, so that we open up in renewed adoration toward our Redeemer Lord, which in turn causes us to rise up to love Him, serve Him, and share Him in whole new ways for all He is.

That's the theme of this book. That's the joyful awakening we invite you to join.

The Subtitles Tell the Story

You hold *CIA*'s "New Revised Version." Hardback, at nearly 470 pages, the original edition appeared in 2003. (You can read it online at *www.ReadCIA.com*). Now, drawing on the extraordinary gifts of my dear colleague, Richard Ross, it's been "reincarnated" at 176 pages.

Cutting out 300 pages, however, is not the most significant development. The modified subtitle is. The original *CIA* had *A Joyful Manifesto on the Supremacy of God's Son*. But this revised *CIA* urges *Join the Joyful Awakening to the Supremacy of God's Son*. Did you catch the shift? Frankly, it's titanic.

A decade ago many parts of Christ's body were sleeping through a major crisis, which I called a "crisis of supremacy" (analyzed in chapters here, as well). To borrow Max Lucado's metaphor, too often Jesus was seen as a computer mouse, readily available to move the cursor across the screen to click on whatever we needed next from God. I wrote my "manifesto" to help call the Church to reengage with the active reign of Jesus—to wake up to who He really is as God's Son, where He's leading in God's purposes, and what He's doing with God's people—across our land and among the nations.

But things are changing. Today this revised *CIA* invites you to expect, prepare for, and even experience something so joyous no Jesus follower would dare be left behind. I call it a Christ Awakening, defined as God's Spirit using God's Word to reintroduce God's people to God's Son for ALL He is.

One evidence of this increased spiritual foment can be found in the titles of books published since 2003, such as: A*bove All Earthly Powers: Christ in a Postmodern World* (David Wells); *Seeing and Savoring Jesus Christ* (John Piper); *The Challenge of Jesus: Rediscovering Who Jesus Was and Is* (N.T. Wright); *Jesus Made in America: A Cultural History* *from the Puritans to the "Passion of the Christ"* (Stephen Nichols); *Christless Christianity: The Alternative Gospel of the American Church* (Michael Horton); *Jesus Manifesto: Restoring the Supremacy and Sovereignty of Jesus Christ* (Leonard Sweet, Frank Viola); *Jesus Ascended: The Meaning of Christ's Continuing Incarnation* (Gerrit Dawson); and *Student Ministry and the Supremacy of Christ* (Richard Ross).

Christ Is Now

Editors for *The Economist* magazine recently authored *God Is Back: How the Global Revival of Faith Is Changing the World*. Similarly, this revised *CIA* might have been renamed: *Christ Is Back: The Awakening of the Church that Will Change the Nation and the World (and All of Us in the Process!)*.

Except, of course . . . our Lord Jesus is not "back." *He never left!* Christ is now. Ascended. Ruling. Redeeming. Triumphant. Moving sovereignly throughout His church. His reign is as undiminished in this hour as it will be the hour we stand before Him at the Climax, in the new heaven and earth. His irrevocable authority needs no reinstatement. Rather, it is we who need restoration. It is the vision of our hearts that needs to replenished, reconquered, and recommissioned in Him and for Him.

For starters, this means we need to revisit *the cross,* the apex of the supremacy of the slaughtered Lamb who rules victorious at the center of the throne (Rev. 5). Our King reigns because He prevailed on the darkest day ever. He reigns because He delivered us from sin and judgment, defeated the minions of evil, depleted death's horrors forever. The impending awakening *CIA* points toward will reintroduce you powerfully to both the *Christ* (heaven's designation for our mighty Monarch) and Him *crucified* (His irreplaceable, royal scepter).

Invitation

Over the years the Holy Spirit used the original *CIA* (and my teachings based on it) to revitalize and equip Christian leaders (mostly) to be "Christ proclaimers" for a Christ Awakening. But a short time ago one of our nation's foremost trainers of student ministry leaders, seminary professor Richard Ross, approached me with a persuasive proposal: to condense, remix, update, and republish *CHRIST IS ALL!* in a format accessible to Christians everywhere (not just leaders), encouraging mass distribution. You need to read Richard's statement at the end of the book to understand the real story behind his dream.

Richard's proposal has now become reality. You're holding it! It's not so much a *manifesto* anymore. Rather, it's more like an *invitation*. An invitation to enter into something worthy of your whole heart. An invitation to join a movement already underway. An invitation to start celebrating, as a way of life, nothing less than the supremacy of God's Son for all He is, for you and for me, for now and forever.

Next step? You might want to RSVP the Father.

(Be sure to read "How to Get the Most Out of This Book." You'll be amazed at what's waiting for you.)

How to Get the Most Out of This Book

This book is so short you can read it in a day. You might even complete it on a coast-to-coast flight.

But think about this: you could also swallow a full bottle of vitamins in one day. If you did, you would experience some value. But most of the vitamins would pass through your system unabsorbed. Or you could take a quick 30-minute walk around the edge of Niagara Falls. But with no time to process what you're seeing, you'd be too overwhelmed by its magnificent grandeur to appreciate adequately the roaring spectacle before you.

My point? You might want to take your time with this book. Like vitamins, it seeks to revitalize your entire walk with the Lord Jesus Christ. Like a falls, it bursts with fresh, even stunning, ways to think about God's Son; it unveils often neglected, unexplored truths of His greatness and glory.

So what might you do instead? Well, for example, you might choose one chapter a day. If you count Richard's statement at the end of the book as one day's reading, there are 27 chapters in all—nearly a full month's worth. Each day, after working through the chapter, take the challenge at the end titled Going Deeper. Read the suggested related passage of Scripture. Then visit *www.ReadCIA.com* and click on the recommended parallel portion from the original, 470-page *CHRIST IS ALL!* This will allow you to expand your thinking on that day's topic. (And, it's free!) Implementing all three suggestions requires 45–60 minutes a day.

Another way for you, the reader, to journey through these pages meaningfully would be with a small group of friends. Visit *www.ChristIsAllBook.com* to download free "Discussion Guide for Small Groups." Talking over each chapter, even with only two or three others on a weekly basis, is an excellent way to go!

In fact, when you visit *www.ChristIsAllBook.com*, you'll find there's a whole lot more to *CIA* than first meets the eye.

For example, you'll uncover more free resources, including a special *CIA* Devotional Guide as well as a series of *CIA* Audio Readings for your iPod or MP3. The site *www.ProclaimHope.com* also provides a wealth of additional free resources to follow up on all God begins in your life while reading *CHRIST IS ALL!* (See the Resources section at the back of the book for more information.)

And if that isn't enough (!), when you go to *www.ReadCIA.com*, click on appendix III, which documents a library full of books that were consulted (at times quoted) in writing *CHRIST IS ALL!*, any one of which might be the next book you should read.

Throughout the book you'll find dozens of "Quotable Quotes." Often the insights given do not fit directly with the topic on a particular page. The reason? Quotable Quotes are designed to help readers keep reflecting on our major themes: who Christ is, what His reign is about, the crisis in how Christians see Him, ways to foster a Christ Awakening. So, when you come to a Quotable Quote, pause and reflect. Then go back to the topic at hand. (And maybe later, share it with someone else!)

Finally, spread it around! The Web address *www.ChristIsAllBook.com* provides an opportunity for you to order the book you hold in bulk, with major quantity discounts, to help you get this book into many more hands. In addition, you'll see there a free sermon outline on "The Supremacy of Christ" based on Colossians. You or your pastor could use it for a Sunday school class or worship service to introduce the *CIA* vision and prepare fellow Christians to receive their own copies of the book as they leave—to join the joyful awakening!

Vitamins. Waterfalls. Christ Awakenings. Some things just work better when given the right amount of time to be absorbed, to be appreciated, and to be embraced.

ONE

Who is God's Son and why does it matter?

At the moment of His Second Coming,
Christ will appear, more majestic and powerful
than we can possibly imagine.
He will split the heavens.
All humanity will see Him for who He is.
Who He will be on THAT DAY is precisely who He is THIS DAY.
His sovereign glory then is His sovereign glory now.
What He will be Lord of then, He is Lord of now.

The question is:
Do we really know Him like that?
The question is:
Does this really matter?

God spoke to our forefathers through the prophets, and He revealed Himself in many other ways. Beginning 2000 years ago He has chosen to reveal Himself most clearly in His Son. This is a perfect plan since the Son is the radiance of God's glory and the exact representation of His nature. When the Son had made purification of sins, He was enthroned at the right hand of the Majesty on high. The Father then announced that in this age of the church God the Son is to have supremacy.

But by the twenty-first century, most believers lost focus on these truths. They still spoke of Jesus, but they mostly spoke of Him concerning the days He walked on earth. They were more likely to picture Him sitting on a big rock with giggling children in His lap than reigning from the throne of heaven. Sermons, Bible lessons, and

1

church hallway conversations became almost completely devoid of any focus on the transcendent majesty of who the Son is today.

Believers, local churches, and Christian organizations that lost their focus on the glory of the Son came to lose hope. This left much of the church lethargic and mostly irrelevant. Many churches became filled with hopeless leaders and members.

Believers generally shifted their primary focus to becoming more prosperous, comfortable, and happy. They still held to Jesus but just as their church mascot and an addendum to pursuing the American dream. Like the frog in the kettle, many believers slowly have lost any sense of the majesty of Christ. Many have slipped so far in their view of Christ that they almost need to be introduced to Him all over again. (Whole chapters here explore this pervasive crisis.)

A New Beginning

Sovereign God always is achieving His sovereign purposes. Just now there is every indication the Father and the Spirit are initiating a movement, waking the church to the reigning glory of the Son. For over 30 years I've watched God move His church toward an unprecedented moment that may now be near. I've witnessed a groundswell toward worldwide revival throughout the church. Today many Christian leaders sense it's truly at hand.

We stand at a doorway. Beyond it beckons a wide-scale awakening to God's Son throughout the body of Christ. It is an awakening for which many have longed and labored for years. We are poised at the sunrise of extraordinary answers to the cries of the modern-day global prayer movement, a movement unprecedented in church history. We rise with the crest of a wave that can lift us into fresh hope, passion, worship, and mission focused on the Lord Jesus Christ.

We are gathered at the launch point of a grand campaign. It is a campaign to proclaim the supremacy of God's Son to Christians everywhere, doing so in such a way that every facet of discipleship, church life, and outreach can be radically (and wonderfully) transformed in the process. As we're about to see in this little volume, what is now required is to flood the church with Messengers of Hope to foster and serve Christ Awakening movements right where they live.

And what comprises Christ Awakenings? The answer forms the foundation for this book, so grab hold of it:

> *A Christ Awakening unfolds whenever*
> *God's Spirit uses God's Word*
> *to reintroduce God's people*
> *to God's Son for ALL He is.*

Within the Trinity the Father Himself is so thoroughly consumed with the primacy of His Son that throughout the New Testament He insists on being known as "the Father of our Lord Jesus Christ." Can we choose to be any less passionate about this same Person?

The Person-Driven Life

Many today call Christians to be "purpose driven." That's good. But think about this: to truly live a purpose-driven life, you must be passion driven because without a lasting passion for the purpose you will not be able to sustain your involvement in the purpose. But before you can be passion driven, you first of all must become promise driven. You need to live with a sense of hope about which you are passionate because you are confident these promises will be fulfilled.

Ultimately you cannot be promise driven unless, first of all, you are Person driven. All of the promises of God are yes to us in the person of Christ Jesus (2 Cor. 1:21), which

> **QUOTABLE QUOTE**
>
> *It pleased God, in His eternal purpose, to choose and ordain the Lord Jesus, His only begotten Son, to be Mediator between God and man, the Prophet, Priest, and King, the Head and Savior of His Church, the Heir of all things, the Judge of the world; unto whom He did from all eternity give a people, to be His seed, and to be by Him in time redeemed, called, justified, sanctified, and glorified.*
>
> (FROM THE WESTMINSTER CONFESSION OF FAITH)

3

means they are fulfilled in Him and only belong to me because I belong to Him.

We become fatigued if we are trying to be purpose driven when we are not, first of all, Person driven. But if we experience an awakening to all Christ is, our new way of seeing this Person creates a fresh sense of promise, a new fire of passion as we move out with His purpose.

What Christ will be Lord of ultimately, He is Lord of already. Ten thousand years from today, who He is as the Son of God will remain exactly the same as it is today. His glory will be no different at that point from what is true of our Savior at this point.

We follow Jesus in anticipatory discipleship. Simply put, we love and serve our Savior at this moment in a way that prepares us to receive more of what He has for us the next moment. Christian discipleship consists in large part of eagerly seeking all God has promised us in the unending reign of His Son and then walking with Christ today in a way that is compatible with what we seek. (Chapter 14 will amplify this theme.)

Any human prospects (Christian or otherwise) that leave Him out of the equation for all He really is must inevitably dissolve into irrelevance, confusion, and despair. Our future is not preeminently about things or events, but about Christ. "For to me, to live is Christ and to die is gain" (Phil. 1:21).

Christ declares, "I am the Alpha and the Omega, the first and the last, the beginning and the end" (Rev. 22:13). Not only was He at the beginning, but He Himself is the Beginning. Not only will He be waiting for us at the end; He is the End. All history streams from Him and is directed toward Him, to be completed by Him. The eternal past has no other eternal future but Christ alone.

A Crisis of Supremacy

There is an emergency, however. Believers in significant numbers already find themselves caught in its grip. It is *a crisis of supremacy*. It signals a serious shortfall in how we see, seek, and speak about Christ. Believers sensitive to this issue are making remarkable and troubling discoveries.

- We have found that references to Jesus Christ, as He is today, are seldom even mentioned inside many churches. They may refer to Jesus' days on earth or even quote Him from that period. They likely use the word *God* often. But they almost never speak specifically of Christ and His reign from heaven as it is unfolding today.
- Many of us have participated in extended worship sessions where specific references to Christ were virtually absent in the choruses we sang.
- Others report listening to widely respected preachers deliver biblically grounded messages that barely referenced our Lord Jesus, let alone bring the congregation to bow at the feet of their King.

How many of us follow Jesus daily with the exciting conviction that what He will be Lord of ultimately He is Lord of even now? That every believer is being led by Him in triumphal procession today toward the Grand Finale over which He will fully triumph at the end?

Without a doubt Christ embodies our blessed hope. He provides the guarantee for all we could ever become or do for God. And He offers to be this for us in Himself alone (1 Tim. 1 and Titus 2). But I ask you: Is this normally, consistently, how we talk about Him with one another?

Such silence and confusion about Jesus form a major part of the crisis of supremacy and help explain the worrisome spiritual malaise that plagues many of our congregations. It provides one solid insight into the various deep-seated disappointments with Christ that eat away at passion for His Kingdom. It is a prime source of growing despair over endless battles with sin and evil.

Over 80 percent of U.S. congregations are either stagnant or dying. In proportion to population there are fewer than half as many churches today as a century ago. In fact, the United States is considered by some to be one of the largest unchurched nations in the world, in a class with China, India, Indonesia, and Japan.

Should not such facts send forth strong warnings? Shouldn't these developments challenge us, at the very least, to reexamine in what ways the glory of Christ Himself is currently misunderstood and miscommunicated inside the church by those who claim His name?

Jesus Our Mascot

As I've taught for years, in so many churches Jesus is deployed as our football mascot. On Sunday we trot Him out to cheer us up and to give us new vigor. We look to Him to reinvigorate our celebration of victories we think we're destined to win. Enthusiasm for Him energizes us for awhile.

But then, for the rest of the week, He is pretty much relegated to the sidelines as our figurehead. We are the ones who call the shots. We welcome Him among us to cheer us on, to inspire our efforts, to give us confidence about the outcome of the contest. But in the end the "game" is really about us, not about Him.

Without promoting an overriding passion for Christ as our Monarch, as our everything, why would we ever openly celebrate Him as anything other than our mascot?

Faded Passions

One of America's best-known worship leaders recently confided to me a personal heartache he faces repeatedly in churches where he ministers: "Often it feels to me as if, for many of our people, singing praise songs and hymns on a Sunday morning has turned into an affair with Christ." I was stunned by his imagery.

He continued: "Too many of us are far more passionate about lesser, temporal concerns such as getting ahead at the office, finding personal happiness in a hobby, driving a new car, or rearing well-balanced children. But we rarely ever get that excited about Christ Himself, at least on any consistent basis. Except when we enter a sanctuary on a Sunday. Then for awhile we end up sort of 'swooning' over Christ with feel-good music and heart-stirring prayers—only to return to the daily grind of secular seductions to which, for all practical purposes, we're thoroughly 'married.'"

He concluded, "Christ is more like a 'mistress' to us. He's someone with whom we have these periodic affairs to reinvigorate our spirits so we can return, refreshed, to engage all the other agendas that dominate us most of the time."

Lost Hope

Unmet longings for promised spiritual advances suggest that Christ somehow has failed us. He has not brought to pass what we have every right to expect from Someone who declares to utterly love us while at the same time holding sway over an entire creation. If truth were told, you and I have probably backlogged scores of prayers for help and healing that inexplicably still remain unanswered.

As psychologist John Eldredge reminds us, such doubts can unleash "the most poisonous" lies in Satan's arsenal. Using them to intensify every other form of hopelessness, the Tempter whispers, "For you personally, things will never, ever change!"

The implications of this are huge. Any loss of hope in Christ *inside* the church wounds our witness outside the church. It guts the credibility of our claims to a deeper spirituality. It significantly paralyzes our mission to neighbors and nations. It reveals to the world that our vision of God's Son is too small.

Your Church's Conversations

Do the Christians in your church ever spend time talking to one another about the supremacy of God's Son (by whatever terms they use)? If so, do they speak in ways that indicate a desire to deposit with one another larger visions of who He is and how He reigns? Whether conversing between worship services, in a weekly home Bible study, or at a Saturday men's breakfast, do the Christians you know seek to promote among themselves greater hope in Christ and His Kingdom? Or do you see a crisis of supremacy at all?

Messengers of Hope

The time is at hand to mount a campaign within the church to reconnect the people of God to the Son of God for all He's worth—to recover all the hope and passion we are meant to have toward Him. We must set about the task of delivering to fellow Christians a radically reformed (though thoroughly biblical) Message of Hope.

God has recruited and empowered millions of passionate believers everywhere. For strategic breakthroughs of His Kingdom purposes, they are committed to inviting Christ to live His life through them at any cost. These pioneering believers are the first wave throughout the church of the promised awakening to Christ we so desperately need.

A Campaign of Hope

A genuine, all-out campaign inside our churches is needed—a campaign for the glory of Christ, to proclaim His name, fame, and reign to fellow believers, to restore their hope and passion toward Christ, a campaign that involves each of us as Messengers of Hope. We must set about the task of delivering to fellow Christians a radically biblical Message of Hope. And we must do so without delay.

The stakes are high, especially in our witness for Christ to neighbors and nations. Only as we carry out a Campaign of Hope successfully *inside* our churches will Christians be able and willing to embrace wholeheartedly our mission outside, from neighborhoods, to the poor, to the earth's unreached peoples.

You can make a decisive difference in your church by what you say about the Savior to disciples who sit with you every Sunday. Invite the Spirit to flow through you as you help others become captivated by hope, living out the promises Jesus secures for them. Then recruit them as Messengers of Hope themselves, equipped to present to fellow Christians a more dynamic vision of Jesus for all He is. Your equipping and then reproducing yourself through others comprises the Campaign of Hope.

I'm convinced such a campaign already is rising in today's church! Come and join in the joyful awakening to the supremacy of God's Son!

GO DEEPER: Read Colossians 1. Explore chapter 1 at *www.ReadCIA.com*.

TWO

Why is spiritual awakening all about the supremacy of Christ?

This Christ Awakening cannot come soon enough. That's because the crisis of supremacy looming before us outweighs all others. It carries repercussions for an entire generation of God's people. It impacts the Kingdom of God and its advance among the nations. It is a crisis of Christology or, more accurately, a crisis of supremacy.

Expanding our definition of *supremacy* will require a significant shift in how Jesus is viewed by many followers. The Scripture points toward much more than what we commonly refer to as the centrality of God's Son. Does that insight surprise you?

Centrality and Supremacy

Scripture points toward much more than what we commonly refer to as the centrality of God's Son. Of course, centrality remains an important biblical concept. It characterizes a whole set of Jesus' lordship claims. It affirms Him as the center of everything, meant to be in the middle of everything, surrounded by everything. And that He is. As Dietrich Bonhoeffer named Him, He is by nature "Christ, the Center." We must never cease to sound this note loud and clear.

> **QUOTABLE QUOTE**
>
> *The American Jesus is more a pawn than a king, pushed around in a complex game of cultural (and countercultural) chess, sacrificed here for this cause and there for another.*
>
> (DR. STEPHEN PROTHERO)

But supremacy takes our vision of Him to a whole new level. Similar to centrality, His claims to supremacy rise from His nature as God's Son. To worship Him as supreme in the universe moves beyond centrality. As supreme, our Lord is not only surrounded by everything, but He also *surrounds* everything with Himself. As Lord, He encompasses all of us within His rule.

Certainly, Christians properly profess that "Jesus is the center of my life." And that's true. But *which* Jesus is at the center of my life? That's the issue. Is it the One whose glory enfolds my life, consumes my life, and defines my life because He alone thoroughly sums up my life—both its meaning and its destiny—and sums it up in Himself?

Here's how Eugene Peterson pictures "supremacy" in his paraphrase of Colossians 1:18 in *The Message:*

> He was supreme in the beginning and
> —leading the resurrection parade—
> he is supreme in the end.
> From beginning to end he's there,
> towering far above everything, everyone.
> So spacious is he, so roomy,
> that everything of God finds its proper place in him
> without crowding.

The Messiah that Christians follow is one who is both central and supreme, both intimate and infinite—a Sovereign who is wholly above us while at the same time wholly among us. This is how the Church today must see and seek Him once again. This is how we must speak of Him once again. If we're ever to recover fully all that His centrality holds for us, we will need to increase our emphasis on the place of His supremacy. Given the current crisis in our Christology, we must do so without delay. The effort must receive our highest priority.

Circumference and Supremacy

Christians, we might say, are like an uncapped bottle cast into the ocean. Once the bottle (the believer) is in the ocean (Christ), the ocean can begin to fill the bottle (representing the idea of centrality). But that's just the beginning of the adventure. There's still the whole Atlantic to explore, into which to plunge, through which to navigate. This represents our pursuit of fuller dimensions of Christ's supremacy for our lives (just as the ocean ultimately surrounds the bottle).

Full of water, the bottle can still be swept by currents out to sea. This pictures a Christian who puts his or her eyes on Christ, seeking His glory and pursuing the manifestation of His kingship in all things, among all peoples. Colossians 1:27 combines both aspects: Christ not only dwells in us (just as the ocean gets into the bottle—centrality), but Christ is also "the hope of glory" for us (just as the bottle flows out to sea—supremacy).

> ### QUOTABLE QUOTE
>
> *The church has become uncertain of Jesus, even uncomfortable with Him. We instinctually sense that the foundation of salvation is in trouble. And it is. Church history is sadly replete with a tendency to forsake Christ. The Church has a long history of discomfort with Christ. The maneuvering of Christ to the margins of our culture—and to the margins of many of our churches—may diminish the status of Christianity (Christendom). At the same time, it also puts believers in a position to experience the transforming power of the gospel in new ways, for the gospel is most empowered when it is least encumbered.*
>
> (DR. JAMES R. EDWARDS)

Not only does the Holy Spirit want to fill our souls with the Living Water, but He also wants to compel our souls to venture forth into the Great Deep of God's eternal purposes in Jesus.

To put it another way, there's a world of difference between saying: "God loves you and has a wonderful plan for your life," and saying:

> "God loves His Son and has a wonderful plan for Him,
> to sum up everything in heaven and earth
> under Him as Redeemer and Lord;
> and He loves you and me enough to
> give us a strategic place in it."

The first promise is about centrality; the second is about supremacy. The second perspective, unfortunately, is the grand reality woefully neglected among far too many Christians.

Missionary statesman E. Stanley Jones understood this larger perspective on Jesus well. He proclaimed the Savior throughout India for 40 years in the 1900s—doing so among multitudes of devotees to Hindu deities. Jones found it necessary to remind Indian Christians that Christ was simultaneously their center and their circumference (or, to use our terms here, both central and supreme). That was something no village idol could claim.

Start with Christ as our center, Jones argued, but then keep moving toward the circumference. However, do so knowing that because He is God and Lord no one should ever expect to reach the "end point" of His reign. "Christ is all infinite and boundless," he declared.

> ## QUOTABLE QUOTE
>
> *Tetlesthai—it is finished! The most significant single word in the Greek New Testament translates to the most triumphant declaration!*
> *It contains both a prophecy and a verdict. On the cross Jesus, the Son, anticipated the Father's verdict and His ultimate intervention. The dawn of the world's redemption had broken, and with it the chains of human slavery to sin, shame and condemnation were shattered.*
>
> (Dr. Jack Hayford)

12

That's the language of supremacy. It is similar to the language of God's Messianic-era promise to Jerusalem in Zechariah 2:5: "I ... will be a wall of fire around her (circumference), and I will be its glory in her midst (center)."

On one hand, centrality calls us to let our lives be wrapped around who Jesus is. On the other hand, supremacy requires that our lives also be wrapped up into who Jesus is. Without question, there is a delightful difference between these two complementary positions!

> *Centrality* is about Christ's right to be kept at the
> center of who we are, where we are headed,
> all we are doing and how we are blessed.

> *Supremacy* speaks of so much more.
> It proclaims Christ's right to keep us at the center of
> who He is, where He is headed,
> what He is imparting, and how He is blessed.

Watch how this distinction emerges in five familiar New Testament texts (and there are many more like them):

- "Christ is all (supremacy), and in all (centrality)" (Col. 3:11).
- "One Lord, Jesus Christ, by whom are all things (supremacy), and we exist through Him (centrality)" (1 Cor. 8:6).
- "I press on so that I may lay hold of that (centrality) for which also I was laid hold of by Christ Jesus (supremacy)" (Phil. 3:12).
- "He who abides in Me (supremacy) and I in him (centrality), he bears much fruit" (John 15:5).

QUOTABLE QUOTE

For nothing counts with God, except His beloved Son, Jesus Christ, who is completely pure and holy before Him. Where He is, there God looks and has His pleasure.

(Martin Luther)

- "Seeing that His divine power has granted to us everything pertaining to life and godliness (centrality), through the true knowledge of Him who called us by His own glory and excellence (supremacy)" (2 Pet. 1:3).

Centrality and supremacy—center and circumference. Any recovery of an abounding hope in Christ among our churches will begin as we're reintroduced to our Savior as *both*. However, if vast numbers of Christians are to use God's Word to call God's people to God's Son for all He is, our word to one another must place the strongest emphasis on His *supremacy*. What a movement to join!

GO DEEPER: Read Isaiah 40:1-11. Explore chapter 1 at *www.ReadCIA.com*.

THREE

How does the supremacy of the Son fit with the Trinity?

Retired talk-show host Larry King was reared in a Jewish home. He remarked once that the one interview he would most like to land is with God Himself. If this happened, he said, he would ask God just one simple question: "Do you really have a Son?" Even talk-show hosts can sense that understanding the Trinity is of central importance.

A Trinitarian Project

Early on I want to affirm my bedrock commitment to the truth of the Triune God. In confessing Christ as supreme, I'm not suggesting that Jesus is all there is to God, that all deity has been collapsed into Christ alone, that our destiny is only about Him. I agree with Timothy George: "What makes God, God? It is the relationship of total and mutual self-giving by which the Father gives everything to the Son, the Son offers back all that He has to glorify the Father, with the love of each being established and sealed by the Holy Spirit, who proceeds from both. The doctrine of the Trinity tells us that relationship—personality—is at the heart of the universe."

Maintaining the supremacy of the Lord Jesus Christ for all eternity—and, in the process, transforming us into people with

> **QUOTABLE QUOTE**
>
> *The riches of Christ are unsearchable (Eph. 3:8).*
> *Like the earth, they are too vast to explore, like the sea too deep to fathom. They are untraceable, inexhaustible, illimitable, inscrutable and incalculable. What is certain about the wealth Christ has and gives is that we shall never come to an end of it.*
>
> (J.R.W. STOTT)

15

Christ-focused purposes—will never cease to be a Trinitarian project. Every dimension of hope is initiated by the Father, developed by the Spirit, while always exalting the Son.

The radiance Christ brings us, as the Son of the Father, is inseparable from the fundamental nature of the Godhead—just as the rays of the physical sun could never exist apart from the sun itself. Ultimately, the uniqueness of His relationship to the Father and the Spirit, rather than His saving mission for the Redeemed, bestows on Him preeminence in everything (Col. 1). Nothing about Christ as the focus of God's promises should ever rob the Father or the Spirit of equal praise.

QUOTABLE QUOTE

He is indeed proved to be the Son of His Father. But He is found to be both Lord and God of all else. All things are put under Him and delivered to Him. For He is God, and all things are subjected to Him. Nevertheless, the Son refers all that He has received to the Father. The Father is the source of His Son Himself, whom He begot as Lord.

(NOVATIAN [c. 235], A ROMAN ELDER AND THEOLOGIAN)

Legitimacy of Christ's Supremacy

As I was waiting to catch a plane, my attention was arrested by the front page headline on a newsstand rack. "He's no 'Son of God'!" leaped from a Minneapolis newspaper. The reporter told of 35 Muslim preachers from the local Islamic Center who fanned out that month to nearly 300 Christian churches and ministries in the Twin Cities to present lectures on their view of Christ.

Their challenge to Christians? Here's how one speaker put it: "The Trinity is merely a human lapse toward polytheism. Christians have become hung up on the Messenger, Jesus, and in the process they have forsaken His message. They should have just stuck with the teachings of Jesus. They should have revered Him as the prophet He is and avoided all the other embellishments."

And I thought to myself: Embellishments? Quite the contrary. From the Bible's point of view, who the Messenger is, in the unbroken fellowship of the Trinity, determines unconditionally the legitimacy and potency of the supremacy He claims and the hope over which He reigns.

Therefore, any message He proclaims is woven automatically into who He is as the Son of God. He is the only Prophet ever to appear among the nations who has focused all prophecies and promises on Himself alone. This is how He brings us to God. No Jesus, no hope. We cannot have one without the other.

The Early Church

The early Church understood this. Confessing Jesus to be Lord, the Church confirmed His divinity by its witness to the full panorama of God's attributes, functions, authority, power, and rights in Him. The adoration of the Son by early Christians (many of whom were previously monotheistic Jews who abhorred idolatry) was unqualified and wholehearted.

Nowhere, observes Donald MacLeod, do we find any debate in the first century over His inherent superiority as God. As far as they were concerned, when Jesus taught, God taught. When Jesus healed, God healed. When He wept, God wept. When He suffered, God suffered. When He conquered, it was the triumphant work of the Godhead. Wherever Jesus' reign broke through, the whole Trinity was on display. Culminated under Jesus as Lord, eternity holds just one additional climactic drama: everlasting worship of Father, Son, and Holy Spirit as the three-in-one.

When men and women surrendered to Jesus to become His disciples, they were initiated into a relationship with the Tri-Personal Being. Even though Jesus claims sole universal authority in Matthew 28:19, still He commands us to baptize His followers "in the name of the Father and the Son and the Holy Spirit." And whenever a promise was fulfilled in Jesus' name, the glory belonged equally to the Godhead who made it all possible, working together as One to bring it about. As 1 Peter 1:2 reminds us, we are chosen "according to the foreknowledge of God the Father, by the sanctifying work of the Spirit, to obey Jesus Christ and be sprinkled with His blood."

The Second Coming

Even in the Consummation, the mission of the Son will be to secure before the whole universe the glory of the Godhead, for the Godhead, in the midst of the Godhead. One day this will come about fully as He will submit Himself (and everything He has conquered), by the Spirit, to the Father's pleasure—just as a devoted Son would be expected to do. Yet even that only can happen once the Father, by the Spirit, has secured for His Son the full recognition of His lordship over everything in heaven and earth and under the earth (compare Phil. 2:5-11 with 1 Cor. 15:20-28 and Rev. 5).

Without qualification (as John records), the Son will prevail steadfastly at the center of the Father's throne, world without end, while the Spirit's fires illuminate Him there, for elders and angels (and all of us) to behold and adore with abandon (Rev. 4; 5; and 21). Permission to live for Him with passion at this very moment springs from the passion that will be required of us when His glory is fully revealed.

He will remain exalted as our Mediator-Monarch, still actively leading us in salvation's saga throughout all ages to come. Christ will continue His role as the new Adam of our race.

Wherever God's inexhaustible grace continues to pour out on the new heaven and new earth, the One who is the "glory as of the only begotten from the Father, full of grace and truth" (John 1:14) will remain at the forefront of the action. He never will cease to be lifted up before the saints so we can worship His matchless majesty. This in turn will bring unending honor to the Father who gave Him up for us all (Phil. 2).

Beyond every other ecstatic enjoyment of the age to come, none will surpass its zenith: Christ's presence, displayed for us to marvel at, welcoming us into encounters with the Living God as a result. We will be enraptured with Christ's glory straight on but unafraid.

GO DEEPER: Read Ephesians 1:1-14. Explore chapter 2 at *www.ReadCIA.com*.

FOUR

What difference should it make that Christ is on the throne today?

On her way home from Sunday School, Wendy announced from the back seat of the car: "I guess God must have made the world with His left hand." Her mother inquired, "Why would you think that?" "Because today we learned that Jesus is sitting on His right hand!" A humorous misunderstanding, to be sure, but one that highlights a beautiful, biblical picture for the high honor God has given His Son.

At the Throne

Who Christ is, at this very hour, seated upon the throne of heaven, makes a world of difference. Because Jesus ascended back to heaven and was enthroned, the active advance of God's Kingdom streams out everywhere. It flows forth from one royal Court, through one royal Person, with incomparable precision of purpose. All of life—whether for individuals, churches, or nations— plays itself out under the immediate, unstoppable, unavoidable (even if unrecognized) sovereignty of the Son of God.

> **QUOTABLE QUOTE**
>
> *Unbelievers do not see Christ as their greatest treasure. Neither do most believers. We live as blind people, chasing after the light we can see—the satisfaction that blessings bring— and not valuing the light we cannot see— the glory of Christ. More is available to us in Christ than we dare imagine. We settle for so much less. We taste Him so little.*
>
> (DR. LARRY CRABB)

19

He is "the ruler of the kings of the earth" (Rev. 1:5).

Our Lord has no serious rivals in the universe. Instead the Father aggressively is uniting all things under His Son's feet this very moment. Christ is not waiting to be crowned as king. He is only waiting to be recognized as king. Reigning as its only Sovereign, He is responsible to judge the world and then cleanse it for His own uses, one way or another (Acts 17).

Even as you read these words, He is actively restoring all creation, according to God's eternal plan, by the increasing subjugation of all things to Himself (Eph. 1). One day earth's peoples from all the ages will be convincingly conquered at Christ's Second Coming. They will be summed up in our Lord forever, either by redemption or by judgment.

Lordship Now

The message of the Christ's enthronement comes down to this:

> What Jesus will be Lord of ultimately, He is fully Lord of now.
> Whatever hope Jesus' reign will offer the universe ultimately,
> it offers believers now.
> All things are as much under His authoritative oversight at this
> moment as they will be in the day of His return.

Even now He freely exercises all of His divine rights, executing divine purposes.

Since Christ's coronation in heaven, according to Acts 1, the church not only looks up (for His return), and looks out (on His missionary advance), but also looks forward (to whatever more of His Kingdom is about to be revealed among the nations). God's Word assures us that in every step of our journey His Son continues extending His scepter, enforcing His dominion, and validating His victories. That's why we have full assurance that our labors for Him will never be wasted. Our mission to earth's peoples is not a fool's errand. In fact, He's actually going before us as we go.

All of this has practical implications for our personal walk with God's Son. Even before the end our union with Him should bring us powerful foretastes of who He will be for us then, when He wonderfully wraps up all history and all creation in Himself. "Christ is in you, the hope of glory" (Col. 1:27)—this one verse links our own experience with the new heaven and earth.

Consequently, as amazing as it sounds, believers are actually invited to experience life-changing "beginnings of the end" ahead of time. In other words, we can expect approximations of the Consummation because He already is ruling. (*Approximations* means we can get foretastes now of the Second Coming. The opening paragraphs of chapter 8 will explain in what way the Second Coming is a *Consummation*.)

True, the end is not yet. But every day we do worship Jesus exalted above, who shows us what the End is all about, preserving in Himself every guarantee that the End will come to pass as gloriously as it has been foretold (see Heb. 2). George Ladd reminds us again that Christ is "the presence of the future." He is the future for which the human race was created. At the Father's right hand the Son provides a "preview of coming attractions"!

Because of our union with such a Savior, the Christian is already abiding, in principle, in the Consummation. And that should change how we tackle each moment we live for Him.

Consider this: Outside the Kingdom, humankind proceeds daily from the present into the future, with little sense (or hope) about what the future actually holds. What other choice do finite sinners

> ### QUOTABLE QUOTE
>
> *If students today primarily know Jesus as a friend who gives gifts, where do you think they got that idea? For good or ill, teenagers closely resemble the spiritual lives of their parents, ministers, and congregations. If most believing teenagers have an inadequate view of the reign of Christ right now, perhaps some of the key adults in their lives also need to be reintroduced to the real Jesus for all He is today.*
>
> (DR. RICHARD ROSS)

have, separated from the living God? However, thriving under Christ's rule the believer begins with the future and works its implications back into the present. This places all decisions, ambitions, relations, and missions in a totally different context.

At the throne right now, the future has been described and decided in a Person! His grace toward believers incorporates key themes of His Grand Finale. That's because He Himself defines those themes—whether then or now—by virtue of who He is, where He leads, how He imparts, and what He receives. In other words, by virtue of His supremacy.

Psalm 110

Psalm 110 is the most frequently quoted or referenced Old Testament passage by New Testament writers. Why, out of all the ancient promises, did the first disciples turn to this ancient hymn time and time again? The answer is obvious. This one text spoke more clearly than most about who they understood their enthroned Jesus to be as He worked in His church. Supremacy, you'll notice, is its central theme:

The LORD says to my Lord :
"Sit at My right hand
until I make Your enemies a footstool for Your feet."
The LORD will stretch forth Your strong scepter from Zion, saying,
"Rule in the midst of Your enemies."
Your people will volunteer freely in the day of Your power;
In holy array, from the womb of the dawn,
Your youth are to You as the dew.
The LORD has sworn and will not change His mind,

"You are a priest forever
According to the order of Melchizedek."
The Lord is at Your right hand;
He will shatter kings in the day of His wrath.

Psalm 110 pinpoints the single greatest reality unfolding around us today. Its drama interprets both the front page of our newspapers as well as the front lines of our mission. No matter how far from the center of divine activity we may seem to be, Christ engages every human domain. He engages kingdoms of finance and commerce, entertainment and education, industry and labor, arts and sciences, rulers and governments.

History is not moving in a vacuum. Before the throne, Psalm 110 tells us, we can watch history pursuing one increasing purpose: to bring about the fullest possible expression of Christ's supremacy, to the farthest bounds of earth, to the greatest extent envisioned by the Father.

Our Chief Prayer Partner

The theme of Psalm 110 is picked up and expanded throughout the book of Hebrews. Jesus' prayers, we learn there, are a primary means of expressing His supremacy right now. Fundamentally, they are how He works out the far-reaching ramifications of His Cross and Resurrection, both for churches and for nations.

Chapter 7 of Hebrews makes this clear. Christ has become a priest on the basis of the power of an indestructible life. He represents a better hope, by which we draw near to God. Because He lives forever, He has a permanent priesthood. Therefore He is able to save completely those who come to God through Him because He always lives to intercede for them.

Poised every moment at God's right hand, our Lord Jesus bears on His heart two things: heaven's promises and the saints' pleas simultaneously mingled together. He presents both to the God of all hope. As our Chief Intercessor, He claims for us the Father's absolute favor. It is due Him as the Son and as the King of all kings. His perpetual priesthood procures for us God's promises for every godly desire, every act of obedient faith, every redemptive mission, every battle with the Devil, and especially for every crisis of supremacy we believers may experience.

But there's more. Because He is supreme, Jesus is also the ultimate *Answer* to all of our prayers. That's why the last prayer of the Bible (Rev. 22:20) simply says: "Come, Lord Jesus." Who He is, in kingly array, will finally bring total satisfaction to every cry of our hearts. His prayers ensure for all of us that the crowning conclusion of our prayers will unfold in Him just as the Father ordained from eternity.

GO DEEPER: Read Colossians 3:1-17. Explore chapter 2 at *www.ReadCIA.com*.

FIVE

How does Jesus sum up the Old Testament's "shadows of supremacy"?

A friend compares the abundance of Old Testament predictions of Christ's supreme place in the purposes of God to an obstetrician's ultrasound. This computer-generated picture provides a pregnant mother the ability to see the child forming in her womb. Viewing shadowy movements on the monitor brings her unexpected excitement, to be sure. The mother-to-be can even take the images home as black-and-white prints.

But after the baby is born, no mother hangs a series of framed ultrasound photos on her living room walls or keeps them in her wallet to show friends. No, after the birth those are immediately replaced by an album full of dramatic photos in living color of the actual child. As meaningful as prenatal images may be, as faithful as they are in predicting something of what the baby will look like, their value is surpassed the moment the infant is enfolded in the mother's arms.

This illustrates the link between God's Old Testament pronouncements and the person born in a stable to sum up all of it in Himself. If we were to blend together the massive number of Old Testament promises, including breathtaking horizons of the coming Kingdom laid out by a score

> **QUOTABLE QUOTE**
>
> *The erosion of Christ-centered faith threatens to undermine the identity of evangelical Christianity ...*
> *real revival and genuine reformation will not be built on flimsy foundations.*
>
> (DR. TIMOTHY GEORGE)

of prophets, what would we have? In the final analysis we'd have a dazzling portrait of the person of God's Son, a vivid description of His supremacy. That's because every vision offered there, without exception—whether of grace or judgment—requires Jesus Christ for its fullest meaning and its grandest completion.

Creation

This is certainly the case when it comes to the abundance of Old Testament reflections on God's glory in creation. Accounts include the vivid dramas that open Genesis, the awesome portrayals that shook Job, Isaiah's visions of natural forces implementing God's judgments, Habakkuk's reassurance that the whole earth will respond with oceans of praises to God, or the many Psalms that tell us, "The heavens are telling of the glory of God ... as a bridegroom coming out of his chamber" (Ps. 19:1, 5). The purpose of these texts was to encourage Israel to ponder nature's witness to the greatness and grandeur of God.

Finally, these time-tested reflections on creation served their maximum mission as they added texture to the meaning of Jesus' supremacy—by whom everything was made and from whom everything gained life (John 1). In the flesh the Savior summed up all the glory to which the heavens testified from the beginning. Drawing on Old Testament understandings of creation's wonders, texts about Jesus such as Colossians 1, Romans 1, and John 1

> ### QUOTABLE QUOTE
>
> *In 1737 I had a view, that for me was extraordinary, of the glory of the Son of God as Mediator between God and man and His wonderful, great, full, pure and sweet grace and love, and meek and gentle condescension. This grace appeared ineffably excellent with an excellency great enough to swallow up all thought and conception.... I felt an ardency of soul to be, what I know not otherwise how to express, emptied and annihilated; to lie in the dust and to be full of Christ alone.*
>
> (JONATHAN EDWARDS ON HIS EXPERIENCE ALONE IN A WOODS IN 1739)

explode with deeper meanings. Creation is "window dressing" for Christ's supremacy.

Shadows of Supremacy

Consider a shadow. Referencing Old Testament customs and traditions, Paul reminded Christians that these "are a mere shadow of what is to come; but the substance belongs to Christ" (Col. 2:17). A shadow usually calls attention to something beyond itself, to the object that casts it. In the end Old Testament hopes suggested the shape of Someone far more vivid and tangible and powerful and eternal than any shadow could be.

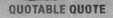

QUOTABLE QUOTE

Christology is the true hub round which the wheel of theology revolves, and to which its separate spokes must each be correctly anchored if the wheel is not to get bent.

(Dr. J. I. Packer)

To borrow a phrase from C. S. Lewis, ancient Scriptures contained the "shadowlands" of Christian hope. Similar to paper silhouettes, Old Testament dramas, personalities, expectations, predictions, types, and themes provided faint but fascinating outlines of Christ and His redemptive mission. In virtually every event and story recorded, using texts found in virtually every book, Christ was previsioned. He was anticipated. But none of these shadows could be adequately understood until the One who cast them was revealed in Jesus of Nazareth.

Covenant promises always were anchored exclusively in the sovereignty of God's own character and actions. But then, "when the fullness of the time came" (Gal. 4:4), they burst forth bodily, revealing unprecedented realities, in plain view of the nations. They sprang into the foreground of world history by the Incarnation of a Savior.

"Jesus' Glasses"

Finally, it happened. Full of Holy Spirit joy, Jesus invited His disciples to step out of the shade into the midday brilliance of His saving mission among them: "Blessed are the eyes which see the things you see, for I say to you, that many prophets and kings (Old Testament) wished to see the things which you see, and did not see them, and to hear the things which you hear, and did not hear them" (Luke 10:23-24).

From that moment it was impossible for believers ever again to study the Old Testament without seeing Christ and His Kingdom permeating its pages. His coming created "Act 2" in redemption's drama. The early Christians uncovered significance in Old Testament passages not apparent to ancient Israel, because now they knew who the story was about and how the story would conclude.

Here are a few examples of what first-century believers saw through "Jesus' glasses":

- He is the new Adam of a promised re-creation, the Overseer of a new race of worshippers to inhabit a new Eden with God's praises (Rom. 5).
- He is the Promised Seed of Abraham, raised up to complete the patriarch's calling to bless all the families of the earth (Gal. 3).
- He is the greater Moses, leading us out of sin's captivity into redemption's eternal inheritance (1 Cor. 10).
- He is the Superior Son of David, bringing with Him an everlasting throne and kingdom that conquers all others (Acts 2).
- He is the Prophets' Prophet, challenging and replacing the status quo not just in one nation but

> ## QUOTABLE QUOTE
>
> *The hope of glory within us reminds us that we have a destiny— that time is marching toward a moment when every knee will bow before the beauty of this One who has saved our souls. This is the culmination of every longing we've ever known, the promise for every death we've endured, the wonder that wakes us each morning with expectation and yes, hope, even amidst the darkest hours of our humanity. Because Jesus is our destiny, once we taste of Him, the hope of glory that lies ahead becomes for us the real life.*
>
> (TRICIA RHODES)

throughout the whole creation (Heb. 1).

- He is the Suffering Servant, who sacrificially bears the sins of His people and then extends through them His redemptive, healing mission to all peoples (1 Pet. 2).

What, after all, did Jesus mean by His oft-repeated claim that everything He did was "according to the Scriptures"? Quite simply, the Old Testament narrative culminated in His person and His triumphs. Its whole plot pivoted on Him. He was the goal of every redemptive initiative launched there.

In the Consummation, Israel had expected to see her vindication before her enemies, deliverance from all suffering, victory over every evil power, restoration to God's full favor, a whole new beginning stretching into eternal ages. But to everyone's utter amazement the end invaded this present age through a Nazarene rabbi. In Himself and by Himself, Israel's destiny was achieved in the truest sense God ever intended. Now those promises await the great day when Christ completes them fully and finally for His people. Isn't it curious how on the first Easter, as Luke 24 reports it, Jesus kept coming back to the ancient foreshadowings?

> Then beginning with Moses and with all the prophets, He explained to them the things concerning Himself in all the Scriptures.... "These are My words which I spoke to you while I was still with you, that all things which are written about Me in the Law of Moses and the Prophets and the Psalms must be fulfilled." Then He opened their minds to understand the Scriptures, and He said to them, "Thus it is written, that the

---

QUOTABLE QUOTE

I must surrender my fascination with myself to a more worthy preoccupation with the character and purposes of Christ. I am not the point. He is. I exist for Him. He does not exist for me. Is there a passion to be consumed with the work of Christ, a passion to know Him as Lord?

(Dr. Larry Crabb)

Christ would suffer and rise again from the dead the third day, and that repentance for forgiveness of sins would be proclaimed in His name to all the nations" (Luke 24:27, 44-47).

Old Testament hope was apparently the agenda most on Jesus mind when He rose from the dead. In this Risen One prophetic history had reached its pinnacle not only for Israel but for all earth's peoples. Now every other promise could unfold.

No wonder those Emmaus disciples, so filled with despair at the beginning of their journey, found their hearts burning within them, "strangely warmed" (as Wesley described it) by the way Christ unfolded for them how the Old Testament was alive in Himself. This same deliverance from hopelessness—this same encounter with the Lord of glory—awaits any of us who allow Him to instruct us "along the way."

GO DEEPER: Read 2 Peter 1. Explore appendix V at *www.ReadCIA.com*.

SIX

How does the Incarnation touch our personal experiences of hopelessness?

Our everlasting hope has been fused to a person who is no less than Immanuel, God with us. God dwells in Him fully and is made fully accessible to us in Him forever. All of God's promises are equally and completely accessible as we receive them in Christ supreme.

Christ's Incarnation not only brought a more comprehensive revelation of our hope but also a new activity by heaven to secure that hope. What He did and said in His earthly ministry revealed the determined strategy of the Father to bless the redeemed eternally. In the days of His flesh, Christ was the hope of the universe, not "on hold" but "on the move."

In Christ the Kingdom was "at hand" (Mark 1). In Him the Kingdom was "coming." He vindicated His words by extraordinary deeds of power, representing early stages of His Second Coming. "But if I cast out demons by the finger of God, then the kingdom of God has come upon you" (Luke 11:20). Therefore, every force of hopelessness gripping His hearers was countered, exorcised, and replaced with Himself.

> ## QUOTABLE QUOTE
>
> *Jesus is not merely the agent through whom the knowledge of God is communicated. He is himself the very content of the communication. Where Jesus is preached, the very glory of God shines through. This God was in Christ reconciling the world to himself.*
>
> (DR. CHRISTOPHER J. H. WRIGHT)

Son of Man

Of all the Old Testament titles Jesus took for Himself, none was used more frequently than Son of Man. And for good reason. Taken from the writings of two Old Testament prophets, it permanently melded themes of Incarnation, supremacy, and hope.

Throughout Ezekiel God used the title to describe the seer's humble position in serving captive Jewish exiles. Borrowing the phrase "Son of Man," Jesus likened His experience to that of Ezekiel's humiliation and sufferings. It recalled for His followers the costliness of bringing hope to captives of sin. Being a son of man pointed to how He emptied Himself of all divine privileges in order to bring spiritual refugees into the benefits of divine promises (see Phil. 2).

But the phrase also appears in the book of Daniel. There, Son of Man describes something different. There we find a human but radiant figure coming on clouds of glory to receive authority over the whole earth on behalf of all peoples (Dan. 7). In a similar way Christ represented His Incarnation as the fulfillment of Daniel's vision. Because He became one of us, a son of man, He also became God's climactic word on the salvation of our race and removing the curse from God's creation.

> **QUOTABLE QUOTE**
>
> *The bottom line here is that Jesus of Nazareth saw himself as the Son of God. Whatever we do afterwards, we must first decide what to do with this. If he was correct, we must fall down and worship him. If he was not correct, we must crucify him.*
>
> (Dr. Donald MacLeod)

Son of Man, therefore, points to Christ's servant role as well as to His sovereignty role in God's eternal plan for the nations. It gives the Incarnation and the Kingdom promises common ground. In fact, it weds them as one and the same. Christ embodied all God's promises in a human life for the first and only time in history.

This is nicely verified in Hebrews 1 when it speaks of Jesus as the "exact representation" of God (v. 3). That word picture comes from Roman gold coins engraved or stamped with the image of the emperor. That image is what gave them their ultimate legitimacy and value. Similarly, we could say that the Servant of God is the "imprint" of God's divine essence. Thus, He became God's "currency" for distributing His promises to His people. Christ sums up magnificently all heaven's blessings and deposits them unconditionally to our account.

But there's more. This Son—to whom all promises point, in whom the whole universe holds together, and to whom has been given every eternal resource one could long for—has thoroughly expressed God's nature as supreme. He did this by becoming a man who conquered every foe, human and spiritual, and then sat down "at the right hand of the Majesty on high" (v. 3) to reign over God's people and impart His grace forever.

Hopelessness and Hope

Unprotected and vulnerable in His humanity, Jesus entered directly into our own painful frustrations. He engaged our precarious conditions, tasted our futilities, and embraced our despairs.

But He entered into our hopeless condition at an even more profound level. He laid hold of that which perpetrated our worst nightmares. By assuming our sin as if it were His own, He endured the penalty of our rebellion against the promises of God and against the God of all promises. In our place He entered the black hole of humanity's most horrifying form of hopelessness. "My God, My God, why have You forsaken Me?" He cried (Matt. 27:46).

Under the judgment of the Cross, He shared our desperate straits, drinking our bitter cup to the end. Amazing grace! He paid the ultimate price to allow us to reenter the heavenly hope we had forfeited, the hope that Scripture calls eternal life. Christ emptied Himself—He donated Himself!—so that in spite of the godless sinners we are, God might bring to pass His consummate plan for the ages through the life-giving reign of His Son.

By taking on human flesh, by abandoning Himself to be the Servant of servants, Christ actually renounced any claim to final control over His own destiny. He humbly placed Himself totally at the Father's disposal. He left in the Father's hands completely the fulfilling of covenant promises. The Son "emptied Himself" (Phil. 2:7) because He chose to wait for the Father to vindicate Him, for the Spirit to raise Him, and for lasting lordship to be bestowed upon Him.

Sealed Promises

To be sure, the glory He received as He ascended on high was the same glory He had with the Father and the Spirit from all eternity (John 17). Still, by lifting Him up out of disgrace, despair, and destruction and by giving Him a name above every other name along with a throne above every other dominion, God sealed irrevocably every promise Christ proclaimed (Eph. 1).

The faithfulness of the Father to the Son incarnate, who surrendered so unconditionally to His will, was ultimately displayed when He presented to Him the nations as His inheritance (Ps. 2). The Son has become the heir of all for which we could ever hope (Heb. 1). Even so, the Father will manifest the same faithful commitment to everyone who sets his or her hope on the Son and "kisses" Him (as Psalm 2 puts it in the King James Version—an act expressing full allegiance to the crown He wears).

The Incarnation provides irrefutable proof that our God is personally committed to the future of humankind. Why? Because, through endless ages a Man, delivered from death, will occupy the praises of heaven—a Man who is at the same time God, One with the Father and the Spirit. As a Scottish theologian once noted: we have hope because "the dust of the earth sits on the throne of the Majesty on High." For the Father to renege on even one of His promises to us is for Him to renege on His promise to glorify His Son.

For the Father to renege on even one of His promises to us is for Him to renege on His promise to glorify His Son. Christ reigns among you, and He is your great assurance of all the glorious things God has for you throughout all the ages to come.

GO DEEPER: Read Isaiah 9:1-7; Zechariah 9:9-13. Explore chapter 7 at *www.ReadCIA.com*.

SEVEN

Why is the Cross the great crossroads for our future?

What was written on Pontius Pilate's sign nailed to the cross above our Savior's head? "This is the *King* of the Jews" (Luke 23:38, author's emphasis). Even then His supremacy bannered His sufferings.

All the wealth of God's Kingdom purposes depends entirely upon Calvary to become reality for any sinner. Therefore, Jesus focused His entire earthly life toward the Cross. There He was able to secure God's purposes for heaven and earth, including each of us.

How overwhelmingly precious is the certainty of our prospect: "If God is for us, who is against us? He who did not spare His own Son, but delivered Him over for us all, how will He not also with Him freely give us all things?" (Rom. 8:31-32). Every promise God has ever issued to the human race is captured by that phrase: "all things."

The Cross is the fountainhead of everlasting bounties to be poured out relentlessly upon grateful saints everywhere, for all time and eternity. So great was the sacrifice of God's Son—so marvelous its ramifications, so extraordinary its accomplishments, and so all-encompassing its consequences—that every other grace the Father has granted is unconditionally guaranteed in the Son.

> **QUOTABLE QUOTE**
>
> *In Jesus Christ the reality of God entered into the reality of this world.... Henceforth one can speak neither of God nor of the world without speaking of Jesus Christ. All concepts of reality which do not take account of Him are abstractions.*
>
> (DIETRICH BONHOEFFER)

The Great Crossroads

Christ's death marks the most critical intersection for a hopeless humanity traveling toward eternal judgment. It's the most authentic "cross-road" there is. On the harrowing hill of execution, just one single day created the historic moment toward which every promise of Scripture to the nations had pointed and from which every promise will reach ultimate fulfillment.

At the foot of the Cross two themes converged. The glories of God was one, including all the streams of His blessings, all the triumphs of His grace, all the manifestations of His majesty, all the grandeurs of His holiness, all the thunders of His judgments, and the all-subduing power of His love. The other theme consisted of deadly dramas dictated by the sins, sicknesses, and sorrows of our rebel race.

Then the Cross provided the pivot point to turn sinners away from the dead end of the latter road and toward a dynamic new destination in Jesus. There He took upon Himself the cancer of our terminal hostility toward God. Through what happened, our Lord provided a way of escape out of darkness to bask evermore in the thick brilliance of divine beauty. If that's not a vision of His supremacy, then what is?

No one ever suffered like the Master suffered. In Himself and by Himself, He penetrated the bowels of mankind's miseries. He drank the bitter dregs of our spiritual ruin. What He endured had unfathomable impact on the powers of darkness. For all the redeemed He absorbed and exhausted and displaced the fatal specter of divine judgment and eternal death.

That's why we call it Good Friday. In place of our alienation, estrangement, and enmity, that bleakest of days opened for all time inexhaustible goodness—so good, in fact, that even former enemies might share in it eternally through union with the conquering Redeemer. He satisfied every condition for fully restoring to us our God-ordained calling.

At the Cross God offered each of us a wonderful exchange:

- My depravity exchanged for Christ's pure righteousness.
- My mortal death exchanged for Christ's immortal life.
- My despair exchanged for a joyous destiny summed up in Him.

- My curse exchanged for eternal blessings that flow from His wounds.
- My judgment exchanged for a safe place inside His Kingdom.
- My defeat and destruction exchanged for His inexhaustible victory.

If Christ's death accomplished all of this, could there ever be any greater display of His all-consuming dominion?

False Hopes

What happened at the Cross permanently exposed counterfeit paths to joy. Calvary was God's masterful stroke of defiance toward rebel dreams. Sacred blood bears witness before all peoples that our own efforts are undeniably in vain. Left to ourselves, all of us are incapable of satisfying either our longings or God's justice. We are confined instead to a cataclysm called eternal death.

If there were any other way to secure our future, then surely Christ's suffering was an insanely tragic endeavor (to paraphrase Gal. 2:20-21). The reality is just the opposite, however. The Cross challenges all peoples to repent of the foolish illusions of our own pomp and power. At the same time the Cross sets before nations unprecedented prospects as bright (and beautiful) as the promises of God—circumscribed by a slain Sacrificial Animal who, at this very moment, is ruling the universe as a Lordly Lion, carrying everything to its preordained Consumation.

Suffering and Supremacy

Where does the suffering of Jesus fit into the supremacy of Jesus? The Cross, in fact, was the definitive display of Christ's eternal dominion. Because of it, slaves of the Fall are liberated. Because of it, Satan's minions are bound. Because of it, death is destroyed, sin is demolished, judgment is absorbed, and fear is banished. If the fruits of the Tree do not magnify the full extent of Christ's kingship, then surely nothing else does.

It is hard to deny a double meaning in Jesus' promise in John 12:32: "And I, if I am lifted up from the earth, will draw all men to Myself." When He promises to "draw all to Me," He's talking supremacy—how the redeemed of all the ages will marshal to Him as willing subjects. When He refers to being "lifted up," He not only pictured hanging on the Cross (as John notes). He also spoke of His Resurrection, Ascension, and Coronation when the Father invited Him up to assume the position He now holds in the universe (Acts 1). Forever, He is the One lifted up to the right hand of God, precisely because of the victory of the Cross, to reign in life over all who surrender to His cleansing blood and saving power.

Ultimately Christ's supremacy does not consist in His ability to impose His will uncontested—to break, or take, or shake things up (all of which He will do one day). Rather, His supremacy is preeminently about His ability to redeem—to reclaim, to reconcile, to restore, to remake, and to redeploy salvaged sinners to serve Kingdom agendas. Therefore, the Cross is really His crown.

In that great day when God's promises in Christ reach their climax, the Cross will still dominate. In the new Jerusalem the victorious Monarch will always be viewed at the same time as a bloodied Martyr.

Therefore, the Cross will forever remain the high watermark of all manifestations of Christ's supremacy. At no point will Jesus ever appear to Christians to be more exalted than when He became the sacrifice for our sin. Nowhere will He ever blaze forth in victory more vividly than when He was vanquished on Golgotha's tree. To worship Him as He deserves, focused on Him as supreme upon His throne, we must learn first to marvel at Him supreme upon His Cross.

GO DEEPER: Read Hebrews 9:11-15, 23-28. Explore chapter 2 at *www.ReadCIA.com.*

EIGHT

In what way do the Resurrection and the Ascension anchor every other hope for us?

In the Resurrection Christ stands unique among all religious leaders of any world religion, whether gurus or prophets. He is the only Master ever to come back permanently alive from the grave, and that by His own power (John 10). In the Resurrection He remains forever unchallenged, utterly superior, and totally beyond the pale of all other contenders.

Christ Is Victor!

When Christ rose to destroy the final opponent to every God-given hope, He swallowed up death itself. Our Lord not only brings us forgiveness by His bloody wounds, but He also frees us by His risen body. He not only cleanses the sin that eternally separated us from God; He also rose to confound, every day in every way, the sin that would enslave and defeat us even now.

Christ is Victor! Let this truth erupt with undying praise to the Triune God. Christ is Victor! Let this truth place our Savior in His position as the heir of all things past, present, and future. Christ is Victor! Let this truth reinforce His role as exclusive source of hope for all humanity.

Christ is Victor! Only this explains why the early Church worshiped Him so fervently, bestowing on Him a vast array of royal titles. Only this vision explains why, despite its ghastly horrors, they celebrated His sacrifice, seeing it as the pinnacle of God's promises. This is where they found courage even in the face of mockery and martyrdom. Filled with the same Spirit that took Jesus out of the tomb, they could not be silent.

Firstfruits of Our Hope

Crushing the jaws of the tomb, Christ became firstfruits—the initial wave—of a future resurrection that lies before us all. We may not yet have the whole harvest, but in Him we hold God's pledge of that harvest. In fact, in Him the harvesting already has begun, with additional (and far more extensive) reaping just ahead (1 Cor. 15).

Out of a borrowed tomb, a new order of existence emerged within time and space. Nothing could be more contemporary than this. It is the inception of a victory that's currently spreading across the earth, destined to envelop everything, everywhere, not long from now.

Anchor of Our Hope

We might say the risen Christ anchors us to all the promises of that new creation. That's what Hebrews 6 concludes. "This hope we have as an anchor of the soul, a hope both sure and steadfast ... where Jesus has entered as a forerunner for us" (vv. 19-20).

Just as an anchor firmly tethers a ship in a storm, even so Christ supreme over the grave holds us, unshakable, to every single dimension of God-given hope. He ties us directly to a future in which "there will no longer be any curse; and the throne of God and of the Lamb will be in it, and His bond-servants will serve Him; they will see His face ... and they will reign forever and ever" (Rev. 22:3-5).

His Resurrection gives us a rock to cling to in life's disillusioning floods and

> ### QUOTABLE QUOTE
>
> *The Gospel-centered community continually encounters and celebrates Christ. Thus, the heart of the Church's evangelistic ministry is its own continuing conversion to the fullness of Christ and His mission. The continual conversion of the Church happens as the congregation hears, responds to and obeys the Gospel of Jesus Christ in ever-new and more comprehensive ways.*
>
> (DR. DARRELL GUDER)

most disheartening storms. It reassures us that when our destiny is consummated in Christ we'll discover that not one of our labors for heaven was ever in vain.

The ramifications of this for today's Christians are breathtaking. It should provide us incomparable, God-concocted cures for every other crisis we face. It should compel us to lose our lives for His sake and the gospel's—to serve the advance of His global cause among earth's peoples—knowing that in the end because He lives we shall live also (Mark 8 with John 14).

Ascended and Enthroned

There's even more! Why was the early Church's vision of the Savior so expansive and so highly exalting? The simple answer: beyond His Incarnation, Crucifixion, and Resurrection, first-century Christians lived daily in the full awareness of Christ's Ascension (Acts 2). Their hearts were set on His coronation and current position at God's right hand (Col. 3). They breathed the air of His active role from the throne of heaven, holding sway as the King of kings and Lord of lords that He already was.

To be sure, Christ inherently possessed the power to govern the universe by virtue of His creating it. In addition, He could claim the inherited right to preside over it because of His death and Resurrection. But now, seated at God's right hand, He had a direct role in the success of His reign due to activities unfolding at His throne every moment. And the early Church knew it because they experienced it.

Ascension Day

Someone has said that the most neglected holy day in the Church calendar is Ascension Day. Multitudes celebrate Christmas, Lent, Good Friday, Easter, and Pentecost. But most of our congregations have given little, if any, thought to the one event when Christ was crowned King of the Universe—that moment, 40 days after His resurrection (Acts 1), when He ascended into heaven to receive a name above every name before which all nations, demons, and angels must bow (Eph. 1; Phil. 1; Rev. 5).

Frequently the Church has been required to choose between two radically different perspectives on God's Son—a choice between a "Christology from below" versus a "Christology from above." Each time the choice was made, the outcome shaped a generation's message about Him and service to Him.

We must, of course, embrace the truths about the humanness—the Incarnation—of Jesus (this is the "below" perspective). But the "above" approach attempts to filter every facet of our vision of the Redeemer (including the Incarnation) through one primary lens: Who He is, at this very hour, seated upon the throne of heaven.

This "above" view invites us to see Him as "God of God"—exalted to the Father's right hand, incomparable in authority and majesty, reigning over earth and heaven—and to regard everything else in this light: worship, prayer, service, fellowship, the gifts of the Spirit, evangelism and missions, lifestyle choices, applications of Scripture, and our struggles with sin.

Some are looking for the time when throughout every Christian tradition we will annually celebrate Ascension Sunday, making as much out of that day as we do out of Christmas, Good Friday, or Easter. Only because of that day does Jesus' Incarnation, Crucifixion, and Resurrection have any permanent redeeming impact.

Some envision Ascension Sunday as not only a day of pomp and praise but also as a sacred season of repentance—a time for turning from specific ways we have reverted (individually and corporately) to treating Jesus as a mascot, a time for calling the church to be reintroduced to Him as our Monarch and, in the process, to recover all the hope in Him we are meant to have. Such will become a way of life for all who join in the joyful awakening that is coming.

GO DEEPER: Read Acts 2:22-39. Explore chapter 2 at *www.ReadCIA.com*.

NINE

Why does the Second Coming project a perfect portrait of our Lord Jesus?

When I was 11, I received an illustrated Bible. The two-page spread picturing Revelation 19—showing a Conqueror clothed in regal robes, seated on a white stallion, surrounded by armies of saints—stunned my unsuspecting heart. This incomparable King was piercing the clouds with the overwhelming radiance of His face, putting His earthly enemies to flight.

I felt something like an electric shock that seemed to travel from head to foot. From that moment the reality of Christ's supremacy, waiting to be decisively displayed in the final battle, molded both my ambitions and my decisions.

Without question the heart and soul of the Consummation will be the renewed vision of the Triune God reflected in the radiance of the triumphant Son. Of the celestial city we read: "And the throne of God and of the Lamb will be in it, and His bond-servants will serve Him; they will see His face, and His name will be on their foreheads" (Rev. 22:3-4).

A Ravishing Vision of the Godhead

In ancient times the Greek word *apocalypsis* (which is used in the Bible to refer to the Consummation or Second Coming) was originally coined to describe a special occasion at the climax of a week of wedding festivities. It was the moment when the veil of the virgin bride was lifted so that the groom and all the guests could finally look upon her beauty. This always took place immediately before the couple slipped away to the honeymoon suite to consummate their marriage in sexual union.

When the book of Revelation calls the Consummation the "marriage supper of the Lamb" (Rev. 19:9), it is borrowing from this ancient tradition. It is pointing us toward that moment when, at Christ's return, we will be ravished together by what lies "behind the veil." Out of this unprecedented revelation of God's glory to us and Christ's finished work in us, we will enter into greater intimacy with the risen Redeemer than we ever dreamed existed.

Christ Will Return

Of one thing we can be sure: at this moment Christ is preparing for something much grander and more conclusive than we can imagine. A revolutionary revelation of His reign is coming when the unbelieving peoples of earth will groan in fear, seeking to flee His face (Rev. 6). Christ will bring down the curtain on the dead-end tragedies of this fallen world, to raise it again on that fabulous forever festival that the Bible terms eternal life.

The Consummation provides one of the most powerful perspectives on the supremacy of Christ. Here's how Paul painted it for a congregation: "For God allowed us to know the secret of his plan, and it is this: he purposes in his sovereign will that all human history will be consummated in Christ, that everything that exists in Heaven or earth shall find its perfection and fulfillment in him" (Eph. 1:10, Phillips).

His Return Essential

All human events, moving under God's sovereign hand, flow toward the appointed hour when Christ's Kingdom will be all that remains. Under Christ's current reign everything is in transition toward the fulfillment of that vision.

Scripture, however, does not encourage naiveté about this goal. We shouldn't project parades of progress or marches moving upward toward the blossoming of some utopian dream. From the Fall forward it has remained clear: history knows no evidence of permanent spiritual progress and no means to reclaim our original innocence by our own efforts.

Enter God's eternal plan! Enter the promises of heaven's choreographed rending of the skies! Like a master surgeon's precise incision, Christ will soon "slice open" heaven and earth to reveal death-defying displays of God's sovereign glory and grace. His Coming will be literal and dramatic. Inescapable. Unavoidable. Utterly transforming.

The nature of evil is such that the end can come no other way. It is absolutely required for Christ to intervene decisively at the close of the conflict of the ages in order to deliver a people helpless to rescue themselves. There needs to be a Consummation. There needs to be an hour when everything is compelled to confess and confirm the supremacy of God's Son!

Fulfillment Expressed in Community

Surrounding the Son in the presence of the Everlasting Father and in the bonds of the Holy Spirit, God's children will enter into a quality of life we might best term "community unity." It is the consummate answer to Jesus' prayer for the church in John 17 as He prayed for oneness.

Following Judgment Day, the Consummation will inaugurate an unprecedented fellowship. The Bible teaches that history's final chapter will introduce one single, world-sized society, comprised of people from every tongue and nation. Together forever, the redeemed will not cease to thrive in the presence of a creative, innovative, inexhaustible, unlimited, and uncontainable God of love.

The Lost

In the "Consume-ation" everyone not consumed with Christ as their Redeemer Lord will be irrevocably banished from His presence. Inevitably the fate of those who permanently reject God's offer to be consumed with Him will be consumed by Christ's judgments. When He comes back, He will be "revealed from heaven with His mighty angels in flaming fire" (2 Thess. 1:7). He will banish into outer darkness those who refuse to participate in the gift of eternal life, abandoned to everlasting weeping and gnashing of teeth (Matt. 25).

This tragedy should make every believer weep. For it will be forever the death of hope for the unsaved. Our desire for the new heaven and earth should increase in us a godly aching for those dearest to us who may never share in that happy day.

His Grandest Coming

When Christ's climactic breakthrough takes place, it will be the grandest of all His comings. It will be the one "coming" that finally and completely sums up every other time He has ever drawn near to His people as Lord!

Without a proper outcome the drama of life easily can become a nightmare for any person. Anticipating our happy ending in Christ, however, takes away fear and frees Christians to enjoy, this very minute, the spectacular story we're a part of—and more importantly, enjoy the Person who makes that story worth living.

Multiple Scriptures predict we will be possessed by His every word, devoured with delight in His majesty, and passionately enthralled with His magnificence. We will be caught up in giving Him unending praise in full view of His throne. (Take a moment to think about that. You will be there to see it!)

The Consummation will not deposit us on some celestial shore where eons crawl by tediously. Instead, the current creation will be both emancipated and renovated by Jesus for our full use. To our joy, themes derived from the initial garden of Eden will be reactivated, though greatly expanded. Creation, liberated from the bondage of decay (Rom. 8), will be incorporated into a new world and a new city sovereignly shaped by the Architect of heaven.

GO DEEPER: Read Revelation 19:11-16; 1:9-20. Explore chapter 3 at *www.ReadCIA.com.*

TEN

How does who Christ is define the *focus* of His supremacy?

Of all the biographies registered in the Library of Congress, one personality has captured the most volumes by a long shot. You guessed it—Jesus. There are nearly 20,000 at this writing, and the number continues to grow.

So, how can we capsulate the hundreds of biblical passages and thousands of studies on Jesus in simple terms that anyone can use to grow a larger vision of Him and His reign? We can consider four dimensions—the *focus,* the *fulfillment,* the *fullness,* and the *fervency* of His supremacy. Our Redeemer is all those things, wrapped into one Person! This chapter and the three that follow will address each of the four dimensions.

Focus

Who occupies the throne that is the focus of the future of the universe? Scripture knows only one answer: our Lord Jesus Christ. Christ supreme! We read: "And I saw ... a Lamb standing, as if slain, ...and the twenty-four elders fell down before the Lamb.... And they sang a new song, saying, 'Worthy are You to take the book and to break its seals; for You were slain, and purchased for God with Your blood men from every tribe and tongue and people and nation'" (Rev. 5:6, 8-9).

Time magazine observed in a cover story: "It would require much calculation to deny that the single most powerful figure—not merely in these two millennia, but in all human history—is Jesus of Nazareth."

An equal indicator of authority is how Christ intends to dominate the future. Just as the course of ages gone by cannot be understood apart from Christ's supremacy, neither can the ages to come. All of God's intentions for the road ahead of us, including the Second Coming, are rooted in the exaltation of Jesus. Understanding this can significantly transform our view of His lordship in general and of His personal involvement with each of us as individuals.

When you balance your checkbook, there comes a point where you have to "sum up" your account. That means you add a number of entries together to get the grand total. Even so, in Christ the promises and purposes of all the ages have been "summed up"—brought to their grand total, unequivocally and irrevocably. Nothing has been left out. Nothing remains to be added to the tally. Jesus sums up all meaning in current reality. He also sums up all outcomes in future reality. He's the source of a New Covenant, a New Creation, and a New Destination—by grace alone, through faith alone, in Him alone. He embodies right now what God's promises will look like when they are fulfilled. Christ is not only the End toward which we move. He is the means to reach that End. Whenever we say, "Jesus is Lord", we are confessing both—that He sums up the End as well as providing the means to it.

> ## QUOTABLE QUOTE
>
> *Jesus is my God, Jesus is my Spouse, Jesus is my Life. Jesus is my only Love, Jesus is my All, Jesus is my Everything. Because of this I am never afraid. I am doing my work with Jesus. I am doing it for Jesus. I'm doing it to Jesus; therefore, the results are His, not mine.*
>
> (MOTHER THERESA)

Jesus asked Peter a penetrating question: "Who do you say that I am?" (Matt. 16:15). Peter answered with the familiar words, "You are the Christ, the Son of the living God" (v. 16). But did he or the others really grasp the full implications of that brief sentence? Based on what many Scriptures teach about the meaning of those two titles—"the Christ" and "Son of the living God"—Peter's response was equivalent to saying:

LORD JESUS ...

You are the Superlative One.
You defy all human categories. No language is adequate to describe You. No analysis can fully record all the roles You must play to advance God's ever-expanding Kingdom (1 Pet. 1).

You are the Incomparable One.
You remain in a class by yourself—no duplicates, no clones. Your importance will continue to eclipse all others, outranking every other being in heaven, earth, or hell. Long after earth's empires vanish, your reign alone will prevail, preeminent, without end (2 Thess. 1).

You are the Exalted One.
For eternity, You will hold the primary focus of our praises, a position of unrivaled distinction, prestige, and majesty in the universe. You will be the joy of all peoples, worthy to receive every treasure, every dominion, and every ounce of praise (Rev. 5).

You are the Preeminent One.
In time, in space, in history, and throughout eternity, You forever lay claim to the universe. As You held the primacy at the beginning ("firstborn of all creation," Col. 1:15), so You will hold it at the end ("firstborn from the dead," Col. 1:18). All things to come are Your possession, to do with as Your Father pleases.

You are the Sufficient One.
Nothing can ever exhaust Your power and resources. You require no outsourcing. You will forever prove totally

adequate for all our longings, fears, needs, or heart cries. You are the final inheritance of each of God's children (Phil. 3).

You are the Triumphant One.

None of Your enemies will prevail. You will defeat all foes unconditionally—both human and demonic—to emerge forever unthreatened, unhindered, and victorious over all opposition, permanently and forever. You are the everlasting Overcomer (Rev. 17).

You are the Unifying One.

Bringing all things under your feet as Lord, You will permanently redeem and reconcile to the Godhead innumerable sinners from all the ages and all the nations. In the Consummation all creation, as well as the Church itself, will be held together in perfect harmony by Your irrevocable decrees and Your indestructible might (Heb. 1).

This breakthrough was the beginning of Peter's own Christ Awakening. On that red-letter day Peter started to discover how His Lord was, in Himself, the focus of everything the Father deserves, desires, designs, and declares. There in Matthew 16, whether he fully grasped it or not, in essence Peter confessed: As Son of God, wherever You dwell, all of God's promises are gathered to You, guaranteed by You, and summed up in You. As Christ You are ordained and anointed as supreme—absolute and universal in every way. You are supreme in the appeal You make to sinners. Supreme in the scope of Your activities on our behalf. Supreme in the depth of Your transforming power for all the redeemed. Supreme in Your reign extended throughout the entire universe. Supreme in the magnificently indescribable future into which You are taking all who are Yours.

In another place the Lord Jesus answered His own question to Peter when He said to John: "I am the Alpha and the Omega, the first and the last, the beginning and the end" (Rev. 22:13). As we saw in chapter 1, not only was He at the beginning, but He Himself is the Beginning. Not only will He be waiting for us at the end; He is the End. All history streams from Him and is directed toward Him, to be completed by Him. Thus Christ and Christ alone can insist on being the One to whom all supremacy belongs.

I like to paraphrase a familiar statement from the brilliant fourth-century African bishop, Augustine:

The one who has Christ has everything.
The one who has everything except for
Christ really has nothing.
And the one who has Christ plus
everything else
does not have any more than the one who
has Christ alone.

This requires our Savior to be both an excluder and an includer. On the one hand, as the Bible testifies, He excludes every other source of hope. There's room for no other. He must exclude all those who choose to put their confidence in any other kind of hope. But, on the other hand, He is also an includer. He includes in Himself every prospect God has for us for the rest of eternity. And He includes with Himself all who trust in Him to receive those everlasting blessings.

Consider the impact of the Salk vaccine which eradicated polio in the 1950s. Once discovered, it rendered all other medicines and therapies for the disease irrelevant (i.e., it was exclusive). But it also became the harbinger of health for anyone around the world who

> ## QUOTABLE QUOTE
>
> *Our research confirms that millions of young outsiders are mentally and emotionally disengaging from Christianity. We are at a turning point for Christianity in America. If we do not wake up to these realities and respond (we risk) losing further credibility.... If Jesus is as valuable as we say he is, then what will we give up for him to remain alive in us? Can we, the Church, spend the next 30 years valuing Jesus Christ and whatever he asks of us above all else? Can we even imagine the what the world would become if we did?*
>
> (DR. JOHN PIPER)

took it in time (i.e., it was inclusive). The unrivaled preeminence of Christ as the hope of the universe is something like that: exclusive and inclusive simultaneously. That's why we say every promise of God must focus on Him and be summed up in Him.

GO DEEPER: Read Psalm 72. Explore chapter 9 at *www.ReadCIA.com*.

ELEVEN

How does where Christ leads define the *fulfillment* of His supremacy?

Imagine an architect enticing a client with blueprints for a prospective office complex. See her using a flip chart of transparencies, placing one design on top of another, gradually exposing how every window, gable, door, and wall will finally fit together to form the desired structure. Eventually the presentation reveals her entire architectural scheme for the new building.

Similarly, as each of God's promises is fulfilled in Jesus, we could say they are superimposed on top of the others. What finally emerges, when all promises are gathered up in their fullest revelation, will be the premiere picture of Christ Himself. God's grand portrait of His Son will become complete at the Second Coming, or what theologians call the Consummation.

Without question, the heart and soul—the apex—of the Consummation will be the renewed vision of the Triune God reflected in the radiance of the triumphant Son. We read: "There will no longer be any curse; and the throne of God and of the Lamb will be in it, and His bond-servants will serve Him; they will see His face, and His name will be on their foreheads" (Rev. 22:3-4). Beyond every other ecstatic enjoyment of the Age to Come, none will surpass its zenith: Christ's presence, displayed for us to marvel at, welcoming us into encounters with the Living God as a result.

Therefore, let me ask you: Based on *all* the Second Coming will reveal our Savior to be—is that the same Person you thought you welcomed into your life when you first came to Him? How comfortable are you with building an ongoing, intimate relationship with the One who will soon climax human history under His sovereign's scepter? Knowing that the same Person who inhabits our lives right now is the same King who will consummate everything in heaven and on earth, do you actually expect to be comfortable with Him anytime soon, let alone *enjoy* Him?

Foretastes

At His ascension Christ's coronation inaugurated the beginnings of the final day. But it did so only in preliminary forms within the unfolding drama of history. Current experiences of Christ's supremacy parallel, but only initially, what we'll behold more fully when Jesus comes back to bring forth a new Jerusalem under His triumphant gaze (Rev. 21–22). All foretastes of the promises wait to be consummated at that hour.

> ### QUOTABLE QUOTE
>
> *If, therefore, all things are put under Christ with the exception of Him who put them under Him, the Son is Lord of all, and the Father is Lord of Him. There is one God, to whom all things are made subject together with Christ, to whom the Father has made all things subject—with the exception of Himself.*
>
> (HIPPOLYTUS [C. 205]
> CHURCH FATHER AND MARTYR)

Where Christ leads shapes the *fulfillment* of His supremacy in two ways. First, the *Consummation*—the glorious climax to history when Christ returns—provides the most comprehensive definition for Christ's supremacy and the hope it brings. Second, this has immediate and exciting *implications* for our walk with Him today, too.

Christ promised us both dimensions in John 14: "I go to prepare a place for you. If I go and prepare a place for you, I will come again and receive you to Myself, that where I am, there you may be also" (14:2-3). "If anyone loves Me, he will keep My word; and My Father will love him, and We will come to him and make Our abode with him" (14:23).

The Consummation Here and Now

Ascended on high, our Redeemer has in one sense already reached the climax of history. He got there ahead of us. The future can now be seen in Him with finality. In Christ the corrupted order of our existence has been replaced with a new order, able to produce fruits of godliness, truth, love. "That which was from the beginning, which we have heard, which we have seen with our eyes, which we have looked at and our hands have touched—this we proclaim concerning the Word of life" (1 John 1:1, NIV).

Because of our union with such a Savior, the Christian is already abiding, in principle, in the Consummation. And that should change how we tackle each moment we live for Him.

When Christ comes at the end of the age, He will not have any more inherent glory than He has at this moment. What He is Lord of ultimately, He is Lord of now. Who He will be in the Consummation is who He is now. If the end is summed up in God's Son, then in a most amazing way the end is with us even now.

As noted in our opening chapter, we're called to live in anticipatory discipleship, obeying Christ in anticipation of all that is to come, seeking to grow a life of obedience and passion for Him that is fully compatible with all God has promised us in the unending reign of His Son. We should do so anticipating increased measures of His sovereign grace at every turn.

> **QUOTABLE QUOTE**
>
> *This judgment will issue eventually in the final denouement of Christ's personal coming from Heaven with the angels of his power. It will bring full justice in dazzling flame upon those who have refused to know God or to obey the Gospel of our Lord Jesus Christ. Their punishment will be eternal exclusion from the radiance of the face of the Lord, and the glorious majesty of power. But to those whom he has made holy his coming will mean splendor unimaginable. It will be a breath-taking wonder to all who believe—including you, for you have believed the message that we have given you.*
>
> (2 THESSALONIANS 1:7-10
> – PHILLIPS TRANSLATION)

Regularly God wants to give us, as individuals and churches, introductory experiences of the Grand Finale. He intends for us to delight in how the Spirit causes Christ's supremacy to invade our daily routines, Christian fellowship, times of worship, or gospel missions at home and abroad. He wants us to taste "the good word of God and the powers of the age to come" (Heb. 6:5) and nothing less!

His Future Return Matters Today

Grasping the Son's impending return can foster unwavering obedience in victorious living now. As Peter writes: "Since everything will be destroyed in this way, what kind of people ought you to be? You ought to live holy and godly lives as you look forward to the day of God and speed its coming.... But in keeping with his promise we are looking forward to a new heaven and a new earth, the home of righteousness. So then, dear friends, since you are looking forward to this, make every effort to be found spotless, blameless and at peace with him" (2 Pet. 3:11-14, NIV).

Biblically speaking, in this age the Spirit wants His church to experience preludes of each theme of the Consummation (including justice, healing, community, worship, and divine presence). In this age every Christian automatically is in the thick of a huge cosmic drama, from creation to Consummation, moving toward victory with every passing day. Christ is both the central plot and the chief character now, the way He will be at the end.

Either the Consummation will reveal how much of this life was spent in indifference toward and even resistance to the reign of Christ; or the Consummation will provide convincing confirmation that our commitment to Jesus was lived in willing response to, and active pursuit of, His lordship in all things (Titus 2).

> **QUOTABLE QUOTE**
>
> *What does the Lord offer in the gospel?*
> *Is it not first Christ, and then all the benefits of Christ?*
> *The Lord Jesus Christ must be received in His whole mediatorial office, as Savior and Lord, as Prophet, Priest and King.*
>
> (THOMAS SHEPARD — PURITAN PASTOR)

Either straw or gold will be found in our hands the day we enter the throne room, the value determined by the Lamb's holy fire (1 Cor. 3). There ought to be sufficient motivation in this fact to drive all of us back to Jesus with a consuming passion for His supremacy right now!

God invites us to enjoy firstfruits of His reign. He intends for us to delight in how the Spirit causes Christ's supremacy to invade our daily routines, Christian fellowship, times of worship, or gospel missions at home and abroad. As we discovered earlier—but it bears repeating—by injecting into the church right now preliminary installments of Jesus' eternal reign, God reveals:

> **QUOTABLE QUOTE**
>
> *If I find in myself desires which nothing in this world can satisfy, the only logical explanation is that I was made for another world.*
>
> (C.S. LEWIS)

What He will be Lord of ultimately, He is Lord of right now.
Who Christ will be in the Consummation is who He is right now.
All the power He will display then is power
that belongs to Him right now.
All the promises He will fulfill then are promises
that are His inheritance right now.
All the glory He will receive from us then is the glory
that is inherently His right now

The fuller revelation of His supremacy that is coming in the Consummation is no more than the full extent of the supremacy that He embodies and can freely exercise right now. Everything Jesus does among us and through us as His people, by the power of His Spirit, is always an approximation of the Consummation.

The "Cosmic Christ"

The Father's intention is that when the Consummation finally breaks upon us the universe will become engaged permanently with Christ and no other. Enter the promises of heaven's unprecedented, choreographed rending of the skies! Enter the fulfillment of Christ's supremacy—climaxing with an in-breaking that will permanently establish His reign in realms both visible and invisible! "God's two creations (writes Christian statesman John R. W. Stott)—his whole universe and his whole church—must be unified under the cosmic Christ who is supreme head of both."

GO DEEPER: Read Isaiah 59:15–60:16. Explore chapter 3 at *www.ReadCIA.com*.

TWELVE

How does what Christ imparts define the *fullness* of His supremacy?

Hundreds of pastors throughout metro New York City, where I live, have banded together for many years in an unprecedented metropolitan prayer movement. Nearly 1,700 churches and 95,000 people have joined forces in hundreds of concerted prayer gatherings. Despite extraordinary denominational and ethnic diversity among Christians in the Big Apple, together we are pursuing our place in God's plans for His Son.

Christ's manifest presence in New York City, especially since the attacks of September 11, 2001, has actually renewed the determination of many to be even more passionate in our prayers and witness. We have discovered an abounding hope for our city that draws on nothing less than a vision of the *fullness* of Christ's supremacy.

Annually, more than 200 leaders gather to intercede for a Christ Awakening in our churches. More than 10,000 believers spend a weekend walking every street of the entire city, praying over every residence and business, asking that the saving glory of Jesus might be manifested in every place.

However, this isn't meant to be the story of New York alone. Christ's empowerment is meant for you, your community, and for believers everywhere. All of us are invited into the fullness of Jesus to live similar lives celebrating our daily experiences of His reign within us and among us.

What Christ Imparts

What does His fullness for us involve? His reign among us incorporates many kinds of approximations of the impending regeneration of the universe—ours to share right now. For example, throughout the New Testament all believers are identified as those currently dead, alive, and ascended *with Christ* (Rom. 6; Eph. 2; Col. 3). It is as if we were already transported to the time of the Consummation and then brought back again. Romans 5 declares that "just as sin reigned in death, so also grace might reign through righteousness to bring eternal life through Jesus Christ our Lord" (vv. 20-21)—meaning that even in this world believers are declared "immortal" in Him, called to live and serve like it.

Separated from Him, dead to God in your sin, at one time we faced no other prospect but dreadful wrath. Only if someone else could bring us alive from the dead, setting us free from the charges against you, could we ever hope to see your precarious condition reversed.

Then one day the gospel came. We believed. Immediately from God's perspective we were raised with His Son from the dead. God reckoned us to be crucified 2,000 years ago with Jesus, at the very time He bore the judgment for our sin (and for all sin) on Calvary.

Long before a new heaven and a new earth ever take center stage, God already has decreed we may walk before Him as if we were a fully resurrected inhabitant of eternity. Such is the unfathomable life God's Son imparts to us.

Justified, we have been declared innocent. Justified, we can rightfully claim to be liberated from all fear toward the Righteous Sovereign. Justified, we remain accepted before the Judge of the universe forever because of our unshakable union with the Judge's Son. Justified, we've become partakers of His holy nature (2 Pet. 1). If this isn't the heart of His supreme "fullness," then what is?

The Holy Spirit

The greatest gift God's Spirit may impart to any believer is simply His sharing with us more of the Son. To be filled with the Spirit (Eph. 5), therefore, means that everything Christ is and offers dwells in us right now (Eph. 3). The Spirit's indwelling presence can be boiled down to one phrase:"Christ in you" (Rom. 8 and Col. 1).

The Spirit is concerned with purifying and setting apart the saints. It's a full-time process. He's consecrating every true believer along three themes of holiness: He is separating us *from* sin, while separating us *unto* Christ, even as He is separating us *for* the purpose of glorifying Christ forever.

Reflecting on the intended impact of the Spirit's ministry, all Christians must ask themselves:

> How does every longing, desire, ambition, and passion the Spirit stirs up within me point me more fully toward Christ and enlarge my hope in Him as Lord of all?

The Church

Between Christ's Ascension and His coming again, the Church not only receives God's promises but is itself a revelation of those promises and how they work, for all peoples to see (Eph. 3). The Church is called to be a preliminary demonstration of what God's Kingdom purposes in Christ will look like as expressed *in community* throughout eternity.

During a time of heightened tensions, with a threat of unwanted schism, a local church asked me to come and help. On the evening I shared my heart with them, I delivered a biblical message on the supremacy of Christ.

Then I took the huge, gold-trimmed, red-velvet pulpit chair that was up on the platform, brought it down below, and put it in the center of the group. Next, all the leaders of the congregation were invited to surround this thronelike structure. Crowded close,

> **QUOTABLE QUOTE**
>
> *The Church of Christ bears witness to the end of all things. It lives from the end, it thinks from the end, it acts from the end, it proclaims its message from the end.... Christ is the new, Christ is the end of the old.... Therefore, the Scriptures need to be read and proclaimed wholly from the viewpoint of the end.*
>
> (DIETRICH BONHOEFFER)

leaders were asked to get down on their knees, as if bowing before a king. In fact, they were asked to envision Christ Himself sitting on the chair in our midst as we held a spontaneous prayer meeting.

After nearly 15 minutes, I had them pray more specific prayers. I asked them to invite Christ to take up His full role among us once again as Head of the Church, Lord of their lives, and Ruler of their congregation. Repentant weeping could be heard among some. Expectant smiles dawned on the faces of others. There was newfound peace among the brethren. Many said afterwards they would never be the same again, or look at Christ the same again, or think about their congregation the same again.

The point made that night was simply this: Jesus is alive, presiding as King, universally available to His Church in the full extent of His supremacy. Therefore, He is able to give powerful expressions of His reign within any congregation whenever we allow Him to draw us together around Himself in community.

Destined to inhabit eternal ages, this new society is already taking shape around our King. Barriers that separate human beings in this age—tradition, race, ethnicity, age, nationality, or cultural and social status—no longer define who Christians are. At the deepest level He unites His people in Himself right now, exactly the way He will when we visibly surround Him in the Consummation (John 17).

Spiritual Warfare

By His death, resurrection, and ascension, Christ's victory over the Devil has already been won. But sinners and demons alike still must

> **QUOTABLE QUOTE**
>
> *There is no standing still in the Christian life. Either we are advancing toward salvation, or we are drifting away to destruction. Drifting is mortal danger (Heb. 2:1). If we do not point our people to the inexhaustible riches of Christ so as to stir them up to go forward into more of God, then we encourage drifting downstream where they will make shipwreck of their faith. (1 Tim. 1:19)*
>
> (Dr. John Piper)

to concede that victory. Though Christ claims full kingship, reigning at God's right hand, He must and will prevail one day as King everywhere. Not only has He inherited the Kingdom, but He must also return in timely fashion to establish it, pervasively, until His dominion obliterates the jaws of Hades itself. In that day the final revelation of Christ's victory over Hell's hoards will be as comprehensive as the rebellion they have waged against Him all along.

For multitudes of mortals as well as droves of demons, the Great Judgment Hour looms ominously. The Judge has been appointed and will carry out with finality every sentence handed down by heaven's court (Acts 17). According to the prophets, however, disquieting spasms of the final battle can be felt already.

Evil is a personal, heavily entrenched rebellion against the living God. We are fighting immense, depraved, and malevolent beings. The successful extension of Christ's reign, first into our congregations and then into our communities and nation, will inevitably whip up whirlpools of resistance in the invisible realm.

The glory of Christ's authority must be manifested in His Church by the power of the Holy Spirit. At the same time all expectations of prevailing in combat depend directly on our willingness to lay down our lives when He asks (Mark 8 with 2 Cor. 4).

Therefore, in Ephesians 6 Christians are urged to wear armor that's fully adequate to the intensity of the spiritual warfare in which we're immersed. Since substantial installments of the Consummate Victory can be expected even today, we should dress like it. Every piece of the armor—belt of truth, breastplate of righteousness, helmet of salvation—represents some aspect of the fullness of Christ that is ours in Him. In His supremacy lies our victory.

> **QUOTABLE QUOTE**
>
> *The light is now shining in the darkness. The followers of Jesus Christ live in the bright interval between Easter and the final great consummation ... living not so much in the last days as in the first days— the opening days of God's new creation. The End came forward into the present in Jesus the Messiah.*
>
> (Dr. N. T. Wright)

One day the armies will confront one another in one grand cosmic conflict. This will usher in a new heaven and earth. Then our hope in Christ will be vindicated once and for all, as we emerge as overcomers (Rev. 2–3). Until then we must wage spiritual conflict using Jesus' sovereign resources. We must do so by the Word of God and prayer (Acts 6), confronting the powers and loving the unredeemed, one skirmish after another—in the fullness of Jesus' name, for His fame, and by His reign.

GO DEEPER: Read Ephesians 1:15-23; 3:7-16. Explore chapter 4 at *www.ReadCIA.com*.

THIRTEEN

How does what Christ receives define the *fervency* of His supremacy?

Listen to these stirring words from the pen of the seventeenth-century Scottish reformer, Samuel Rutherford. After years of persecution and imprisonment for preaching Christ, he wrote from a jail cell that he still found it necessary to pray one major request for himself every single day: *"Lord Jesus, come and conquer me!"* What did he mean by this?

To survive and thrive in his lifelong mission, Rutherford knew one thing was necessary: he must experience daily personal renewal in a manner similar to how Christ's kingship would one day renew all things. The magnitude of sacrifices this cleric had to make for his Scottish people demanded that Christ's majesty constantly dominate his vision.

The reformer needed to be regularly subdued to Christ Himself—*conquered,* as he put it—in a manner reflective of how His Lord would conquer the universe in the grand Resurrection. He knew this alone would preserve His *fervency* for Christ's supremacy.

The same is true for all of us. A comprehensive vision of our ascended Lord Jesus, ruling and active, transforms our hope in Christ into a consuming fervency (passion) for Christ.

Created for Passion

Since Christ is the heir of every promise God has given us, how could any commitment to Him require any less than consuming passion? Paul urges us in Romans 12:11-12 (NIV): "Never be lacking in zeal, but keep your spiritual fervor, serving the Lord. Be joyful in hope." '

Listen to how Jesus fosters fervency for His supremacy:

- "If anyone wishes to come after Me, he must deny himself, and take up his cross and follow Me. For whoever wishes to save his life will lose it, but whoever loses his life for My sake and the gospel's will save it" (Mark 8:34-35). Consuming passion.
- "If anyone comes to Me, and does not hate his own father and mother and wife and children and brothers and sisters, yes, and even his own life, he cannot be My disciple" (Luke 14:26). Consuming passion.
- "Whoever loses his life for my sake will find it" (Matt. 10:39, NIV). Consuming passion.

At this moment Christ longs to incite increased homage toward Himself to intensify our daily obedience to His purposes.

None of this should catch us by surprise. From the beginning our Father created all of us, young and old alike—body, soul, spirit, will, intellect, emotions—to be passionate for His Son. We must never be afraid to give ourselves up to Him with unqualified abandon. Nothing about the Christian life can ever be dubbed as dull while following a Master who marched out of a graveyard to ascend the throne of the universe.

Christ's Passion for Us

On the Cross Christ was consumed with His vision for my destiny to display His glory. I thrive in the wake of the Suffering Servant who, with heart and soul, embraced to His own demise the totality of my desperate plight in order to rescue me from oblivion (Isa. 53).

What is to be my response to His deep devotion to me? I must be willing to experience the same kind of consuming passion for Him. I must be willing to value wholeheartedly the same joy He embraced, the same glory for God He died to vindicate, and the same Kingdom advance over which He reigns.

The Father and the Spirit's Passion for the Son

The full measure of our passion draws upon something else equally profound: how the Father is consumed with infinite love for His Son. He is thoroughly caught up in promoting among the redeemed the adoration His Son deserves.

The Father longs to lavish on us fervent affections that originally He reserved for His Son. "In love he predestined us to be adopted as his sons through Jesus Christ, in accordance with his pleasure and will—to the praise of his glorious grace, which he has freely given us in the One he loves" (Eph. 1:4-6, NIV).

As the Spirit inhabits believers, He makes possible for us to experience the unbounded affection shared within the Godhead. The nearer He brings us to Christ, the larger our King and His dominion appear to us. This unending encounter—this Spirit-induced spectacle—is hope's magnificent obsession.

Consuming and Consumed

"Consuming Christ" speaks of intense, hope-filled longings that never go away, the opposite of the complacency that makes a heart temporarily satiated by the world's deceptive delicacies. Rather, consuming Christ leads to increased hunger to see, seek, and savor more of Him and His blessings upon our lives. It keeps us greedy for God, desperate for God's promises to become reality in our walk with Jesus.

> **QUOTABLE QUOTE**
>
> *Hail, gladdening light, of his pure glory poured*
>
> *Who is the immortal Father, heavenly, blest,*
>
> *Holiest of Holies, Jesus Christ our Lord.*
>
> *Worthiest art thou at all times to be sung,*
>
> *With undefiled tongue, Son of our God, giver of life, alone!*
>
> *Therefore in all the world thy glories, Lord, they own.*
>
> — OLDEST COMPLETE HYMN IN EXISTENCE FROM THE 3RD CENTURY, USED WHE FAMILIES LIT LAMPS AT EVENIN

"Consumed with Christ" is the other side of a passion incited by our hope in His Kingdom. But what does this mean?

Consider how a man and woman consummate a marriage. Though they exchange their vows in front of many witnesses, they seal those vows privately in a profoundly meaningful way by sexual union—an unforgettable exchange of nearly total abandon of two bodies and souls to each other, an unconditional giving of everything that's precious with no holding back.

Christians must not hold back. We must consummate our commitment to the Lord Jesus Christ, to become more intimately involved with Him. Daily we must embrace Christ as our Bridegroom, abandoned to every hope of glory He holds out to us.

A Christ obsession always will call Christians to a purpose beyond themselves. It will point to a passion for God's promises that takes us somewhere, that results in strategic, decisive action to advance the work of Christ's Kingdom.

Unlike the deadly fate of a moth drawn to the warmth and beauty of a candle flame, the closer we get to our Radiant Redeemer the greater our joys, the more energized our labors, the more enticing our prospects—the more alive we will feel! Proverbs 23:17-18 (NIV) proclaims: "Always be zealous for the fear of the LORD. There is surely a future hope for you, and your hope will not be cut off."

Passionate Believers

Although I have moved five times, each time I've prominently displayed a plaque on a wall of my office. It frames a favorite prayer from the African theologian and bishop, Augustine. It exposes

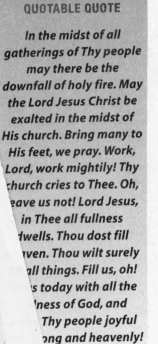

QUOTABLE QUOTE

In the midst of all gatherings of Thy people may there be the downfall of holy fire. May the Lord Jesus Christ be exalted in the midst of His church. Bring many to His feet, we pray. Work, Lord, work mightily! Thy church cries to Thee. Oh, leave us not! Lord Jesus, in Thee all fullness dwells. Thou dost fill heaven. Thou wilt surely all things. Fill us, oh! us today with all the fullness of God, and Thy people joyful among and heavenly!

(CHARLES SPURGEON)

art of passion, a passion fueled by a vision of Jesus as Lord. It come a lifelong prayer of longing for me. Maybe it represents prayer, as well:

You called, you cried,
You shattered my deafness.
You sparkled, you burned,
You scattered my darkness.
You shed forth your fragrance,
And I drew in my breath.
And I pant for you.

Using more contemporary phrases, psychologist Larry Crabb challenges Christians to respond with similar passion when he writes the following (which I formatted in blank-verse style):

To every cry from your passion-filled hearts,
God replies, "Christ."
Let your passion to explain
become a passion to know Christ.
Let your passion to be right
become a passion to honor Christ.
Let your passion to heal
become a passion to give hope.
Let your passion to connect
become a passion to trust a sovereign Christ,
who will do for you exactly what needs to be done.

Passionate Congregations

The senior pastor of the world's largest church shared with me a most fascinating answer to this question: Is there one biblical text that summarizes how the explosion of Christ's work in your congregation came about? He responded: "One passage defines better than most others the kind of people that make up many of our 700,000 members." He read to me Matthew 11:12 (NIV): "The kingdom of heaven has been forcefully advancing, and forceful men lay hold of it."

"Mirroring God's forceful efforts to promote His Son's glory," he said, "true seekers of God's purposes display a similarly aggressive spirit toward the cause of Christ. Seizing God's Kingdom mission, they grab onto His sovereign initiatives and go with Him. Within my own city this passion has taken the form of thousands of cell groups. They pray for, and reach out to, nearby friends and neighbors to bring them to Christ. That's how we've grown from 100 to nearly three quarters of a million in just 40 years!"

The good news is that every congregation has been redeemed for this same kind of adventure, not necessarily in terms of numbers but certainly in terms of dynamics. Such passionate churches are not necessarily more spiritual. They are simply more convinced that since Jesus reigns God is always ready to unveil exciting expressions of His promises in Christ for those "laying hold" of His global cause.

GO DEEPER: Read Philippians 2:5-13; 3:7-16. Explore chapter 5 at *www.ReadCIA.com.*

FOURTEEN

How can hope in Christ's supremacy enrich Christian discipleship?

To hear the hope, share the hope, and grow the hope, we must remain victorious in the hope, learning to walk in the hope. This happens best by practicing *anticipatory discipleship*.

Atheletes training for the 1984 Olympics were forced to experience something akin to anticipatory discipleship. Because of the American boycott of the 1980 Olympics in Russia, American Olympians had to postpone competition for eight full years! Having prepared since 1976 for the Russian Olympics, they were forced to press on for an additional four years of training to stay in shape for the 1984 Olympics in Los Angeles.

Strive to Thrive

Imitating Olympian training, anticipatory discipleship shapes every aspect of Christian obedience. We keep our eyes on the Prize! Anticipatory discipleship *integrates* the promises of God into our walk with His Son. Hope in Christ inspires and intensifies our desire to serve Him because we expect Him to prevail.

The concept of anticipatory discipleship was suggested by our Lord in His original invitation (Mark 1:17): "Follow Me" (His call to discipleship) "and I will make you become fishers of men" (dramatic changes promised). In other words, obedience to Him today could *anticipate* significant transformations tomorrow.

If we have this outlook, it enriches everything from developing qualities of Christlikeness, to worshipping God with abandon, honing hallmarks of holiness, standing with the poor, and increased missionary outreach because we know we are moving from here to there. Every step sets the stage for even more of Christ's reign to break through for us, our churches, our communities, and our generation.

QUOTABLE QUOTE

(God) has now, at the end of the present age, given us the truth in the Son. Through the Son God made the whole universe, and to the Son he has ordained that all creation shall ultimately belong. This Son, radiance of the glory of God, flawless expression of the nature of God, himself the upholding principle of all that is, effected in person the reconciliation between God and man and then took his seat at the right hand of the Majesty on high— thus proving himself, by the more glorious name that he has won, far greater than all the angels of God.

(HEBREWS 1:1-4 – PHILLIPS TRANSLATION)

But unfortunately most church members simply strive to *survive*. Little is anticipatory about much that passes for discipleship. Ours is more "maintenance discipleship" with efforts to remain respectable church members, fulfilling basic biblical obligations, and maintaining morally respectable uprightness.

Pregnant with Promises

A mother-to-be easily is motivated to take on whatever disciplines, diets, schedules, exercises, and precautions would help ensure delivery of a healthy child. She fully cooperates with her doctors; she rarely complains. As each day brings her closer to the due date (the hope for which she endures), she takes additional steps to be ready for the marvelous event.

Even so, Jesus' followers are "pregnant" with promises as big as the Kingdom of our Savior. In a real sense the Holy Spirit "overshadows" God's people to conceive in them and birth through them ministries for Christ that are holy (Luke 1). Like a mother-to-be with her doctor, every serious disciple seeks to give our Lord full cooperation as He brings forth the advance of His Kingdom.

Hope in Christ's Supremacy and Repentance

For the Christian, repentance acts as the hinge of hope. It swings us from destruction, despair, and defeat toward all the promises offered under Jesus' reign. It shifts us from self-absorption over to the joyful state of "Christ-absorption."

Repentance is not a synonym for self-loathing. By it we embrace the truth of our sinful depravity on the inside, to be sure. But repentance prepares us to be seized by the hope-filled vision of Christ's majesty on the outside.

One approach of repentance draws on what I call "the principle of compatibility." The more we get to know Christ for all He is, the better able we become to spot those areas (habits, words, priorities, sins, activities, relationships, possessions, character traits, etc.) that are not really compatible with Christ in His supremacy and so need to be rejected, reshaped, replaced, or redirected.

Why so often do we not see the level of ongoing repentance we know we should experience as Christians? One major reason: we have not been saturated sufficiently with the grand and glorious hope in our Supreme Savior that can inspire such a response. Too often the Christ we proclaim *to one another* is simply too small to make us want to turn from sin and toward Him.

Hope in Christ's Supremacy and Worship

We worship more accurately and more passionately when we do so out of our hope in Christ. After all, He is not only the God who is and was but also the God who is to come (Rev. 1).

Properly understood, worship is designed not only to be Christ focused but also eternity focused. Our worship can prepare us for, and even approximate, the worship we expect to experience in His presence for ages to come. Worship among the nations is actually a preview of an hour not long from now when people from every tongue, tribe, and nation will shout their redemption before Him who sits on the throne (Rev. 5).

True worship, therefore, must stir up in us greater determination to extend His praises right now among friends or neighbors or unreached peoples. All evangelism is ultimately about expanding eternal adoration for God's Son into the midst of those who do not yet know Him.

Hope in Christ's Supremacy and Scripture

Biblical scholars suggest that the Word of God may contain as many as 7,000 separate promise statements. If so, ultimately each one is focused on establishing the preeminence of God's Son. Accordingly, each promise can help "color in" the thrill of anticipatory discipleship. Worship, Scripture, possessions, evangelism, reconciliation, church activities, righteous living, world outreach—all of these find new meaning in the context of God's promises that are "yes" to us in Christ Jesus (2 Cor. 1:20).

We must uncover in God's Word everything we can about the four dimensions of Christ's supremacy: who He is as the Son of God, where He leads in the purposes of God, how He imparts the resources of God, and what He receives from the people of God.

It has been said: God cannot lead us on the basis of facts we do *not* have. Think about this: As we grasp a biblical vision of Jesus' greatness and glory, we will discover a hope we may never have considered previously. Immediately the Spirit will have new possibilities to work with—potent facts in our hearts by which He can take us further with Christ than ever before.

Hope in Christ's Supremacy and Congregational Life

Love is the hallmark of any congregation where Jesus reigns. Maybe the most telling demonstration of such love is this: responding to someone here and now in a manner reflective of how I would expect to show that person my love if we were both suddenly standing together in glory, in the final hour, in full view of the Savior on His throne. One day that is precisely what will happen to both of us! Should I not determine, therefore, how Jesus would expect me to love people there (in *that* day) and then strive, under His lordship, to show them no less of a love *now* (even though I fall short of that goal many times)?

Christ's supremacy also should impact how congregations are led. One church begins every staff meeting by placing an empty chair in the middle of the room. They call it the "Jesus chair." As they begin in prayer, the staff declares to the Father that, as far as they are concerned, His Son occupies that "throne" for the rest of the meeting.

From that point on, they refuse to lose sight of the chair and of the presence of the Lord who is in it. They see Christ as the One for whom the meeting is taking place, the One who is guiding all decisions, and the One prepared to lead their church where they have never gone before (and never would, if left to themselves).

If there's any point in church life where hope in Christ's majesty enriches us corporately, it is Sunday morning (the "first day of the week" celebrating His victory over the grave for all of us). What would happen if every week—based on the singing, the prayers, the Scriptures, the sermon, the whole atmosphere—members left your sanctuary fired up with Kingdom vision, eager to walk into the next six days looking for increased displays of Christ's dominion around them? What if, as a result, people returned the next Sunday full of reports on where they had witnessed revelations of Christ's supremacy—in their lives, or others' lives, or even among the nations?

> **QUOTABLE QUOTE**
>
> *Just as surely as it is appointed for all men to die, and after that pass to their judgment, so it is certain that Christ was offered once to bear the sins of many and after that, to those who look to him, he will appear a second time, not this time to deal with sin, but to bring them to full salvation.*
>
> (HEBREWS 9:27-38 – PHILLIPS TRANSLATION)

Hope in Christ's Supremacy and Finances

Anticipatory discipleship empowers us to reevaluate the extent of our financial obligations. We ask: How do my giving patterns—to my church, to ministries, to missions, to the poor—reflect the supremacy of Christ?

- In what ways does my philosophy of consumption tie into what I expect to be doing with Jesus 10,000 years from now?
- What financial choices made today might free up funds to help promote greater "approximations of the Consummation" where I live? For example: By serving the homeless? By comforting the sick? By lobbying for social change such as prison reforms?
- What material sacrifices should I be willing to make in order to help proclaim Christ's redemptive reign among peoples currently beyond the reach of the gospel?
- How might some form of renouncing or redirecting earthly treasures help me more effectively see, seek, and speak about the supremacy of God's Son?

Simplicity of Christian lifestyle rises best out of a discipleship full of anticipation. It allows us to stay unencumbered and flexible enough to respond adequately to all the new directions God may take us.

Hope in Christ's Supremacy and the Battle with Sin

All sin detours believers from fully engaging Christ for all He is. But hope in Christ supplies an effective antidote to the deceitfulness of sin. Hope motivates us for holy living by reminding us of our ultimate destiny when Jesus will fully reveal Himself to be our all in all, leaving sin powerless to counteract.

Of course, the battle with sin forces us to tackle evils of other kinds such as social injustices, poverty, corporate greed, religious scandal, moral relativism, political oppression, or domestic terrorism. Proclaiming hope in Christ to the poor, for example, must be coupled with efforts to overcome poverty at its systemic roots. Christ's battle call includes a healthy combination of both telling and showing the full extent of His supremacy.

Hope in Christ's Supremacy and Battles with Satan

To avoid any spirit of trivial triumphalism, let's be clear on one thing: Christ's global cause not only initiates harvest fields; it also instigates battlefields. Not every moment in the service of Jesus' Kingdom offers visible, unalloyed advances in His mission. Forces of Darkness are opposed to God's promises, ready to fight them, and us, to the death.

Still we can boast in our undiminished hope. Though the time of their full destruction awaits the Consummation, God's Son is rapidly rendering principalities and powers ineffective and unproductive. He is upholding His cause to bring saving hope to sinners everywhere (compare Rev. 12:1-12 with Heb. 12:25-29). The increased martyrdom of Christians over the past century alone, in unprecedented numbers, only serves to reinforce how decisively and effectively Christ's redemptive mission is penetrating enemy territory.

Hope in Christ's Supremacy and His Global Cause

If, as Christian leaders today are urging all across the globe, "the whole Church must take the whole gospel to the world," it is equally true that to mobilize this groundswell, the whole church must awake to the *"whole Christ"* and to the hope we have in Him for the final outcome of our mission.

According to Jesus the end will not occur apart from the completion of the missionary task (Matt. 24). The One who waits to come back wants to be expected among all peoples when He returns. Therefore He must be proclaimed throughout all the earth as the supreme hope for all peoples—starting right where we live.

Christ's global cause gives primacy to the planting of churches among the thousands of unreached people groups. Missionary leaders today talk about "a church for every people and the gospel for every person." Every newly established congregation becomes a base of operations from which Christ can extend His scepter among those who do not yet know Him (Ps. 110).

Hope in Christ's Supremacy and the Poor and Oppressed

The fact is, over the centuries missionaries compelled by the hope of Christ's supremacy have been found rooting again and again for the oppressed, the disenfranchised, the unreached. With the Consummation as their touchstone, these laborers have tackled down-to-earth realities even as they preached the gospel of eternal life. They defended the poor. They fought for moral and social transformation. They opposed evils like slavery, widow burning, and infanticide at every turn. They emerged as walking revolutions. They themselves became approximations of the Consummation. Why can't the same happen again in our generation?

Hope in Christ's supremacy is the greatest gift we can bring to the poor and oppressed. The gospel of the Kingdom heralds how Christ's reign will one day consume forever all economic poverty and human subjugation, along with injustice, illiteracy, tyranny, sickness, and disease to and all spiritual darkness. The poor need to hear that and hear it now. They also need to be summoned into communities of disciples where they can experience preliminary installments of their Sovereign's liberation as they begin to labor side by side with renewed confidence for increased justice and social reform where they live.

Recently my wife witnessed this truth firsthand in India when she visited with a particular subgroup

> ## QUOTABLE QUOTE
>
> *One of the Elders said, "Don't weep. Look—the Lion from Tribe Judah, the Root of David's Tree, has conquered.... There, surrounded by Throne, Animals, and Elders, was a Lamb, slaughtered but standing tall.... And they sang a new song: Worthy! Take the scroll, open its seals. Slain! Paying in blood, you bought men and women, bought them back from all over the earth, bought them back for God. Then you made them a Kingdom, Priests for our God, Priest-Kings to rule over the earth.... The slain Lamb is worthy! Take the power, the wealth, the wisdom, the strength! Take the honor, the glory, the blessing!"*
>
> (REVELATION 5:5-6, 9-10, 12 – THE MESSAGE)

of Dalits, the self-named Untouchables numbering nearly 200 million. Born into the occupation of latrine cleaning, the Bhangi Dalits had no way out because of the Hindu caste system, that is, until the gospel restored to many hope and dignity. Thousands have turned to Christ. They are experiencing His reign in the most practical ways—including education, hygiene, retraining and community transformation, along with worship and discipleship. Hundreds of new churches planted among them have sustained this wholesale spiritual and social people-movement. Even the Indian government has been forced to take notice of the significant benefits.

Our task as "world Christians" is to infect people everywhere with desires that can only be fulfilled in Jesus, so that they turn to pursue Him with all their hearts. Our privilege is also to enlist lost ones—including the poor, and especially the poor—to participate with Him in God's future, laboring with His people toward the Final Victory.

For Starters: A Morning Worship Discipline

Consider the possibilities offered by the following daily discipline. It's arbitrary, but for the moment view it as training wheels for a child's bike. Learning to ride requires the devices for a time to keep one's balance. Before long they no longer will be necessary.

Build—For six minutes a day, using Scripture primarily, build your own vision of hope in the supremacy of God's Son. Review some of the scores of texts that look at our God-given hope. (See *www.readcia.com* for suggestions.) Consider how each one ultimately exalts Christ. At the same time, don't hesitate to make use of supplementary literature (such as this book) to help open your eyes and reform your view of Christ.

Pray—For five minutes ask God to unleash His promises in greater ways for you and for others, both now and in ages to come. Pray particularly about some of the perspectives you uncovered reading God's Word and/or other Christ-exalting literature.

Strategize—For four minutes a day reflect on how you might combine your hope in Christ more fully with one particular area in your walk with Christ. In other words, apply what you discovered the first six minutes, and prayed about the next five minutes, to some practical dimension of discipleship. Then go out to make it happen the rest of the day.

Proclaim—For three minutes a day share with another Christian the hope in Christ you've uncovered that day as you studied it, prayed over it, and incorporated it into your walk with Him. You could be a Messenger of Hope by writing a Christian friend a brief note, by phoning someone to give a short report on what God is teaching you, or by striking up a quick conversation with a friend at church or on the job. Many can be Messengers of Hope by sharing a growing hope with one's family around the evening meal.

Listen—For two minutes a day sit quietly at the feet of your Lord Jesus. (This might work best at the close of the day.) In absolute silence let your King speak into your heart by His Spirit. Keep this question in mind: What more has the Father revealed in my life this day of the glory of His Son and the work of His Kingdom? Take one minute to write down a thought that best summarizes God's work in you that day.

Twenty minutes a day. That's just ten hours a month. But notice, in the end it adds up to a 120 hours a year! Ask yourself: All other things being equal, between now and a year from now, if I were to add to my life 120 hours of this kind of spiritual growth, what kinds of delightful changes might I expect in my vision of Jesus, my hope toward Him, and my service to Him?

GO DEEPER: Read Mark 8:27–9:8. Explore chapter 12 at *www.ReadCIA.com*.

FIFTEEN

In what sense do we view Jesus as a mascot more than a monarch?

I attended a high school that is football crazy. This Ohio institution has produced 22 state championship teams. The team is the Massillon Tigers. Our mascot requires a taller student to dress up like a tiger— I mean, wearing a real tiger skin! He inherits a name of affection: Obie the Tiger.

Here's how a mascot works. At times, in the midst of a game, if we're falling behind, the coach signals time-out. Because the crowd needs to be stirred to cheer more enthusiastically for the team's victory, the uniformed tiger runs his stripes onto the field. Seeing Obie doubles the crowd's determination to celebrate the champions we hope to be. After all, we are the Massillon Tigers!

In turn, this reinforces the team's confidence in themselves. They charge back to the scrimmage line ready to put bold plays into action, to redouble the struggle, to win the game on their terms. At every succeeding time-out, the mascot reappears, paws lifted triumphantly toward the skies. The roar of the crowd goes up once more. The team regains courage and resolve.

But at each appearance, interestingly, Obie's performance is brief. Then he disappears, sent to the sidelines, put on hold until the next setback. He has served his useful purpose well. We're so proud of him. Everyone feels better now. The game can proceed with new momentum.

In the final analysis the tiger never really gets involved beyond reigniting cries of confidence, beyond giving us an identity to boast about. To be sure, Obie stirs up a certain kind of passion. But it is not really about him. It's about the team and even more about the fans. The team designs the plays, runs the patterns, throws the blocks, reaches the goal, claims the credit. The fans jump with joy, declare their superior skills over the losers, and boast that they are "the Massillon Tigers." Then we all go home satisfied.

Now here's the kicker: What happens the moment our team hits a losing season? What good is the mascot then? The zeal it inspires suddenly feels hollow, even foolish. We are left with little else but embarrassing thoughts of our team's helplessness and hopelessness. Then our passion quickly heads south—for Obie, for our team, for our future, for the game itself.

Jesus the Mascot

In many churches, I fear, Jesus is regularly deployed as our mascot. Once a week on Sunday, we "trot Him out" to cheer us up, to give us new vigor and vision, to reassure us that we are "somebodies." We invite Him to reinforce for us the great things we want to do for God. We look to Him to reinvigorate our celebration of victories we think we're destined to win. He lifts our spirits. He resuscitates our souls. He rebuilds our confidence. He gives us reasons to cheer. He confirms for us over and over that all must be well. We're so proud of Him! We're so happy to be identified with His name. Enthusiasm for Him energizes us for awhile.

Then, for the rest of the week, He is pretty much relegated to the sidelines as our figurehead—the name by which we take the field and the one we call on when we get behind. But for all practical purposes we are the ones who call the shots. We implement the plays, scramble for first downs, and improvise in a pinch. Even if we do it in His name, we do it with little reliance on His person.

Our cheers may be for Him, but our victories are for us. There's scant evidence that we think of ourselves as somehow utterly incapable of doing anything of eternal consequence apart from Him.

This may be the most descriptive (and most disturbing) of all the weak visions of our Lord. We welcome Him among us to cheer us on, to inspire our efforts, to give us confidence about the outcome of the contest. But in the end the "game" is really about us, not about Him.

Promises of fuller displays of His dominion leave our daily discipleship unfazed. We evidence little desperation for increased manifestations of His majesty among us.

Admired and Ignored

As contradictory as it may seem, many of us have redefined Jesus into someone we can both admire and ignore at the same time! To be our mascot, we've redesigned Him to be reasonably convenient—someone praiseworthy, to be sure, but overall kept in reserve, useful, "on call" as required. Rarely does it cross our minds that the supremacy of Christ means that He is the game in the final analysis.

Without promoting an overriding passion for Christ as our Monarch, as our everything, why would we ever openly celebrate Him as anything other than our mascot? The truth is, Jesus' claims to the monarchy make Him the opposite of an Obie character. Instead, He encompasses in Himself the coach, quarterback, playbook, team, uniforms, cheerleader, goalpost, and final championship—the whole nine yards wrapped up in one person alone.

> **QUOTABLE QUOTE**
>
> *We have preached ourselves, not Christ. We have preached too often so as to exalt ourselves instead of magnifying Christ, so as to draw men's eyes to ourselves instead of fixing them on Him and His Cross. Christ, in the sufferings of His first coming and the glory of His second, has not been the Alpha and Omega, the first and the last, of all our sermons.*
>
> (HORATIUS BONAR)

Does our vision of His lordship take on such exalted dimensions inside the Church? Does it express such grand themes? Does it promote an exclusive love for Him—an enthusiasm not unlike what rises from thousands at a Super Bowl—a zeal for His glory evident in our daily routines in the marketplace as much as in our church schedules on weekends? Is the Spirit truly having His way with us?

I suspect we have found far more fascination with the church game itself—with how we are playing it and whether we are winning—than we have with the One in whose name, and for whose sake, the "game" exists at all. Which may explain the reports: Tens of thousands of congregations are wrestling with a leveling off of financial giving, with a growing shortfall of laborers, and with an atmosphere of apathy toward evangelism, compassion ministries, and the global mission of Christ's Kingdom.

Good News

But the good news is this: if we turn back to exalt once again in our Savior as the Monarch He is—if we spread this grander message about God's Son to God's people, inviting them to rediscover in His reign all the hope we are meant to have—we can create a life-saving paradigm shift inside the Church. We can trigger a reignition of our passion for Him as Lord of all. This effort can help bring an end to our scandalous stumblings over Christ's supremacy. It can return us to the dynamics of a Monarch-driven discipleship.

The team has no existence and no reason to exist apart from Him. From Him, through Him, for Him, under Him, in Him, and to Him are all things. And all the fans in the stadium must bow at His feet before they dare to cheer in His name.

GO DEEPER: Read I John 1:1-4; 2:18-25; 4:1-6. Explore chapter 6 at *www.ReadCIA.com*.

SIXTEEN

In what sense is Jesus missing in the American church today?

There is an emergency. A host of believers already are caught in its grip. It is a crisis, a crisis of supremacy. It signals a serious *shortfall* in how we see, seek, and savor God's Son for all He is. In turn, this leads to a *shortfall* in how we speak, show, serve, and share God's Son for all He is.

Believers sensitive to this issue are making remarkable and troubling discoveries. As we put it in chapter 1:

- We have found that references to Jesus Christ, as He is today, seldom are even mentioned inside many churches. They may refer to Jesus' days on earth or even quote Him from that period. They likely use the word *God* often. But they almost never speak specifically of Christ and His reign from heaven today.
- We have participated in extended worship sessions where specific references to Christ were virtually absent in the choruses we sang.
- Others share how they have listened to widely respected preachers deliver biblically grounded messages that barely referenced our Lord Jesus, let alone bring the congregation to bow at the feet of their King.
- We have monitored the between-session conversations of delegates at major Christian conventions, hoping for even a hint that God's Son was somehow vital to their discussions, only to be disappointed time and time again.

That causes me to ask: How many of us follow Jesus daily with the exciting conviction that what He will be Lord of ultimately He is Lord of even now? That every believer is being led by Him in triumphal procession today toward the Grand Finale over which He will fully triumph at the end?

Without a doubt Christ fulfills our everlasting future. He embodies our blessed hope. He provides the guarantee for all we could ever become or do for God. And He offers to be this for us in Himself alone (1 Tim. 1; Titus 2). But I ask you: Is this normally, consistently, how we talk about Him with one another?

Is our most pressing spiritual ambition simply to "flee from the wrath to come" (Luke 3:7)? Or is it much more? Is it also to seek the glory of the One who is to come (1 Thess. 1)?

> ### QUOTABLE QUOTE
>
> *Too many Christians and churches in America have traded in spiritual passion for empty rituals, clever methods and mindless practices. The challenge to today's Church is not methodological. It is a challenge to resuscitate the spiritual passion and fervor of the nation's Christians.*
>
> (DR. GEORGE BARNA)

Confusion and Crisis

Such confusion about Jesus forms a major part of the crisis of supremacy. It helps explain the worrisome spiritual malaise that plagues many of our congregations. It provides one solid insight into the various deep-seated disappointments with Christ that eat away at passion for His Kingdom in so many of our people. It is a prime source of growing despair over endless battles with sin and evil.

Without an adequate view of the incomparable majesty of our Redeemer King, Christians quickly revert to the role of spiritual "couch potatoes." We survey God's purposes in Christ remotely. We're involved with Him at arm's length, at best.

This disquieting discrepancy has blindsided far too many believers around us. It has preempted the vitality of our worship, prayer, community life, and ministry outreach. Above all, it has robbed God of His rightful praise through His people among all peoples.

John tells us: "Anyone who goes too far and does not abide in the teaching of Christ, does not have God" (2 John 9). Period. No exceptions. Could anything be more debilitating for the global cause of Christ than this verdict? Even Christians can renege on living out before the world the implications of His supremacy.

Let's lay it on the table. How many Christians do you know who are fully alert to God's Son for ALL He is in the glory of His supremacy? How many Christians in your congregation may require, in fact, a *reintroduction to Him* on a number of fronts?

If our churches are experiencing the "crisis of supremacy," we must not run from it. It's far too critical. We must expose the ambivalence God's people harbor regarding who we seek, why we seek Him, and how and where we expect to find Him.

Identity Crisis

Many in today's church wrestle with the ultimate *identity crisis,* a disturbing confusion about Christ's identity. Many in our congregations suffer needlessly from insufficient exposure to the Grand Hope we are meant to have in God's Son. Too few disciples are growing in their knowledge of "Christ in you, the hope of glory" (Col. 1:27).

Among the emerging generation of younger American Christians, researchers have uncovered a shift from rational, logical, systematic outlooks on spiritual realities to longings for experiential, mystical engagements with the divine. Diminishing discoveries about Christ's dominion have often led by default to a more me-centered approach to Christianity.

In a nation infatuated with Jesus—actually with many Jesuses distilled from a rainbow of cultural impressions—is the real Son of God the one most Christians follow here? Our historically unprecedented religious diversity has tempted far too many U.S. believers to "pick and choose" from a spiritual smorgasbord piled high with Christian and non-Christian delicacies.

In chapter 1 we rehearsed how 80 percent of U.S. congregations are either stagnant or dying. With every passing year there are approximately 3,000 fewer churches in America than there were the year before. In proportion to population, there are fewer than half as many churches today as there were only a century ago. In fact, the United States is considered by some to be one of the largest unchurched nations in the world—in a class with China, India, Indonesia, and Japan.

Should not such facts send forth strong warnings? Shouldn't these developments challenge us, at the very least, to reexamine in what ways the glory of Christ Himself is currently misunderstood and miscommunicated inside the Church by those who claim His name?

Studies estimate that nearly every Sunday morning a majority of sermons heard across America are centered on daily survival issues rather than Christ's Kingdom issues. Too frequently we propagate among ourselves a gospel that fails to get beyond immediate remedies for hurting hearts, failing families, or troubled communities. Too infrequently do our messages summon hearers passionately to pursue Christ Himself for all He is worth.

Such an outlook eventually produces spiritual hypochondriacs. Christians demand a regimen of churchly remedies to make life more bearable—guaranteeing the enhancement of personal relationships, the development of human potential, or the healing of the "inner child." These believers settle for spiritual sedatives that never can ignite a pursuit of Christ for who He is, what's on His heart, and where He is headed. The gospel has been transformed into a commodity, with the local church acting as the retail outlet, while members are seen as customers.

Inviting People to Christ

Did the message you heard at the beginning of your walk with Jesus captivate you with the righteous reign of Jesus, both for you and for nations? Or was it more about the possibilities of personal fulfillment through the addition of a Savior to your life? Did it announce to you a supreme Lord in whom everything in heaven and on earth is to be consummated, who therefore has every right to consummate your life in Himself and His purposes? Or was the offer more akin to news about a good God who was ready to help you get a good life?

When we invite people to Christ, do we inadvertently imply that they need only come to Him as far as they feel the need to come? Do our offers of God's grace unwittingly encourage others to exploit Christ for their own agendas? To interpret Him essentially as someone at their disposal for their own benefit?

When I encourage someone to "invite Jesus into your heart," is it possible that in doing so I actually create a personal crisis of supremacy for her or him? What if a person unconsciously concludes from this phrase: "Jesus in my heart makes Him more readily available to me, as required to meet my needs, under my supervision, so things don't get out of hand"? No one would ever admit this out loud, of course. But for all practical purposes many have settled for a safer Savior, a manageable one designed to make Him easier to cope with.

Self-Serving Views

Oh, how we have trifled with the Son of God! For all practical purposes our self-serving messages about Him have domesticated Him in our own eyes. We have marginalized Him among His own people. We have sanitized the Son of God! We've settled for sleepy, sentimental, scaled-down versions of the One who reigns supreme. We seldom see Him as Lord over creation, over history, over the Church, and over all the ages to come. Seldom do our hearts and minds get intrigued with Him above everything else.

May God forgive us! We're plagued with a whole spectrum of self-serving messages that put out the fire of our passion for Jesus. To name just a few, we've redefined the Lord Jesus Christ as:

- Our handyman—seen as a source of "quick fixes," to deal with our adversities by providing instant solutions on command.
- Our interior decorator—contracted to embellish and enhance everything we do in the arena of church activities, giving it that "extra something" that always makes our efforts feel so special.

- Our EMT (emergency medical technician)—poised on standby, ready to be brought in at those points where we have finally exhausted our own ingenuity and resources, especially in our determination to do something important for God.
- Our personal trainer—kept on retainer, like our favorite golf coach, to provide practical pointers from time to time so we can play the game of life a little more successfully.
- Our pharmacist—putting healing balm on hurting hearts or prescribing salves for the suffering that life throws at us.

Each of these trite Christologies holds an element of truth, to be sure. Of course Jesus is available for emergencies. Of course He can transform everything we do for the Father into something beautiful. Of course He trains, cures, and inspires. Yet each of these taken alone betrays the scope of the hope God gives us in Christ's glorious greatness.

The Cross

Above every other concern this chapter has addressed regarding self-serving, shortsighted messages of Christ, surely the most grievous is this: the Cross itself gets trivialized by every one of them. Every superficial view of God's Son distorts the testimony of Calvary. Our witness to one another about the wounds of Jesus ends up being weakened and wounded itself, rendered ineffective. We must return to the message of the Cross—to the passion of the Christ—if we're ever to restore our passion for Him and reaffirm our hope in Him for ALL He is. Describing one form of his own zeal for his Lord, Paul exclaimed: "I have been crucified with Christ; and it is no longer I who live, but Christ lives in me; and the life which I now live in the flesh I live by faith in the Son of God, who loved me and gave Himself up for me" (Gal. 2:20). For him the Cross was inseparable from heart-and-soul fervency for Christ's supremacy!

GO DEEPER: Read 2 Corinthians 10:1-6; 11:1-4, 13-14; 6:14-18. Explore chapters 6 and 8 at *www.ReadCIA.com*.

SEVENTEEN

Where do you see the crisis manifesting itself in your church?

In Denmark, Norway, and Great Britain, kings and queens mostly are highly favored figureheads, kept around for ceremonial purposes. But they have no final authority over day-to-day activities in government or the marketplace. Similarly, in some churches Jesus gets feted Sunday after Sunday, highly praised and cheered. Displays of devotion toward Him rarely linger into Monday, however. Church members engage Him too seldom on a daily basis as the One who holds the destiny of all nations and before whom every life stands or falls.

How about the members of your church? Are they captivated by His Royal Highness? Or for all practical purposes has He evolved in their thinking into someone much more akin to a figurehead? Observing their daily walk with Him, what would you conclude?

Would you say your church's small groups major more on helping members *grapple* with challenges in daily living or with helping one another *grab hold* of the hope Jesus on His throne brings to

> **QUOTABLE QUOTE**
>
> *An enterprise which aims at the evangelization of the whole world in a generation, and contemplates the ultimate establishment of the kingdom of Christ, requires that its leaders be Christian statesmen— men with farseeing views, with comprehensive plans, with the power of the intuitive, and with victorious faith.*
>
> (JOHN R. MOTT)

us? Too often we've encouraged one another to incorporate Christ into our lives when and where *we* feel the need for Him. But more often than not, God's Son finds Himself discounted when it comes to expectations regarding decisive displays of His dominion over our everyday experiences.

Your Church' Conversation

Sunday after Sunday how much of the general conversation in your church actually honors Jesus in a manner comparable to how Paul talked and wrote? How often do members say to one another words like these:

- "For to me, to live is Christ and to die is gain" (Phil. 1:21).
- "We proclaim Him, admonishing every man and teaching every man with all wisdom, so that we may present every man complete in Christ" (Col. 1:28).
- "For I determined to know nothing among you except Jesus Christ, and Him crucified" (1 Cor. 2:2).
- In our times of fellowship are we "taking every thought captive to the obedience of Christ" (2 Cor. 10:5)?

> ### QUOTABLE QUOTE
>
> *In reality the church in America is not booming. It is in crisis. The renewal and restoration of the American church must begin with an awe-inspiring encounter with Jesus, the crucified, resurrected and ascended Messiah and Lord.*
> *That central focus on Jesus is critical to the health and growth of missional churches.*
>
> (Dr. David Olson)

In other words, do the Christians around you ever spend time talking to one another about the supremacy of God's Son (by whatever terms they use)? If so, do they speak in ways that indicate a desire to deposit with one another larger visions of who He is and how He reigns? Whether conversing between worship services, in a weekly home Bible study, or at a

Saturday men's breakfast—do the Christians you know seek to promote among themselves greater hope in Christ and His Kingdom?

Too many of us, I'm afraid, have become comfortable simply conversing about benign concepts of God. We allow ourselves to sidestep deeper encounters with Jesus as Lord. Yet there's no getting around the fundamental principle of Romans 10:17: "So faith comes from hearing, and hearing by the word of *Christ*."

This process is as true of *believers* as it is of unbelievers. What Christians hear about their Savior from one another, as a steady diet, determines a good deal of the depth of hope and passion they express toward Him.

Listening Tour

You might want to conduct a "listening tour" at your church. Do it over the next three Sunday mornings. Consider inviting your pastoral staff, elders, or deacons to join you in this experiment. Here's how it works:

When you get to church on Sunday, instead of conversing with people, just listen to them. Walk throughout the building overhearing what people are saying to one another in the fellowship hall, parking lot, sanctuary, and Sunday school classes.

> **QUOTABLE QUOTE**
>
> *Your real new self— which is Christ's and also yours, and yours because it is His—will not come forth as long as you are looking for it. It will come when you are looking for Him.... Give up yourself and you will find your real self. Submit to death, death of your ambitions. Submit with every fiber of your being.... Keep back nothing. Nothing in you that has not died will ever be raised from the dead. But look for Christ and you will find Him, and with Him everything else thrown in.*
>
> (C. S. Lewis)

After three weeks debrief the experiment with your leaders by discussing two questions: (1) How frequently did we hear the name of the Lord Jesus Christ mentioned in conversations the past three Sundays? (2) If we did hear His name, did we ever witness one

We look at this Son and see the God who cannot be seen.
We look at this Son and see God's original purpose in everything created.... Everything got started in him and finds its purpose in him....
He was supreme in the beginning and—leading the resurrection parade—he is supreme in the end.
From beginning to end he's there, towering far above everything, everyone....
All the broken and dislocated pieces of the universe— people and things, animals and atom— get properly fixed and fit together in vibrant harmonies, all because of his death, his blood that poured down from the cross.

(COLOSSIANS 1:15-16, 18, 20
– THE MESSAGE)

believer sharing with another believer something he/she recently discovered about the worth and wonder of the reigning Christ in order to build up the other person's hope and passion toward Him?

Most likely you will be shocked by your findings. As have thousands of other leaders who've tried this experiment, you'll probably discover that God's dear Son, for whose sake a congregation exists in the first place, is rarely mentioned in normal exchanges, even when we're all together as His followers on a Sunday morning.

Your findings will provide proof there is a disturbing drought of biblical vision and passion for the Lord Jesus among the Lord's followers. It is real. It is serious. It is spiritually debilitating. And now it is here. The church's loss of hope and passion toward Christ may well be traced back to how we chatter on about everything else but rarely pause to draw one another into the larger vision of the supremacy of God's Son.

If we fail out of ignorance, indifference, or self-consciousness to speak about the great glories of our Lord Jesus Christ among ourselves as Christians, why should we be surprised so few of us ever dare to speak about Him to the unbelievers around us? We've had little practice doing it with one another. Little effort has been made inside our churches to proclaim Jesus' majesty in order to increase a vision for His preeminence among ourselves.

Just Imagine

But what if every Sunday morning the conversations within your congregation were full of Christ—adults and young people eagerly sharing what they are regularly discovering of the One in whose name we gather, because of whose reign we exist, and for whose fame we live?

What if every time we're together Christians exhorted or challenged one another, warned or comforted one another using freshly uncovered insights into the "unfathomable riches" of God's Son (Eph. 3:8)? Over time how might such consistent conversations lead toward a spiritual revitalization of your church family, possibly quickening a Christ Awakening movement among us?

Among a significant core of disciples, especially within the younger generation, a renewed hunger to feast on deeper biblical teaching about the glorious greatness of Jesus has appeared. More than ever I hear the cry of Christians to be mentored by leaders who refuse to settle for shallow solutions to the crisis. Many are asking to be led into fuller encounters with Christ's glory. They also want to be equipped to proclaim the wonders of His reign to others.

We must accelerate this "movement of messengers." Christians must choose to commit to bringing a fresh message of Christ and His supremacy to other Christians right where they live. If we don't act, the gulf that currently exists—the one between the majesty of

> ### QUOTABLE QUOTE
>
> *Christ is just as much a king when He is waiting as when He is winning! He is just as much king in His ascent as He will be at His descent. He is just as much in control in heaven as He will be on earth.... Christ is not just above any other name (or any other god) in space, but He is above them in power, authority and victory.... The day will come when the only king whom God recognizes will be acknowledged by every tongue ever created.*
>
> (DR. ERWIN LUTZER)

God's Son and the church's loss of hope and passion toward Him—will only grow wider and more ominous.

We need not despair. At this very hour Messengers of Hope are rising up everywhere to meet the challenge. Each place I visit I find Christ proclaimers emerging inside all kinds of congregations and Christian ministries. These witnesses are key both to revival in the body of Christ and to a worldwide acceleration of the gospel of Christ. Is it possible that you are among them?

GO DEEPER: Read Hosea 1:10-11; 2:14-23; 3:4-5. Explore chapters 7 and 8 at *www.ReadCIA.com*.

EIGHTEEN

Where do you see the crisis manifesting itself in you?

Searching for success in all the wrong places frequently deflates devotion for the One whose dominion alone can assure success the way God measures it. A poll by the Barna Research Group asked Americans what they believed was necessary for them to have a successful life. Health? Happy children? Occupational achievements? Only one out of every 14 adults said that anything related to spirituality or faith in Christ would help achieve what they might term success. Is it any wonder many Christians have lost their passion for God's Son?

What about You?

Consider these questions slowly and thoughtfully:
- Who really is the Christ to whom you were converted in the first place?
- Do you sense that He truly conquered your heart that day, the way a King of kings has every right to do?
- Do you sense that as reigning Lord He still maintains full sway over you right now?
- Are you convinced all the promises of God are really and truly summed up in His Son?
- Or do you still struggle with hopelessness?
- Do you know Him as trustworthy, as the One on whom you can depend without reservation?
- What kinds of practical differences does this make in your daily walk with Him?

- How has He, to any depth, become what Paul meant by "Christ in you, the hope of glory" (Col. 1:27)?
- Do you daily expect Him to work in you above and beyond what you have received from Him thus far?
- What do your answers tell you about the "state of hope" in you?

Crisis and Fears

Fears can provide faithful barometers indicating how infected we are with the "crisis of supremacy"—how seriously we have disconnected from the truth about God's grace and glory in Jesus. I've had to confront three major fears. Time and time again they have resurfaced in my struggles to rebuild a more Person-driven (rather than panic-driven) discipleship:

1. The fear that He WON'T.

This is the fear that Christ will not want to break through for me in the ways His supremacy promises, thus leaving me confused, disillusioned, heavyhearted, or ashamed. I fear the potential failure of ever experiencing His supremacy in my life.

2. The fear that He WILL.

This is the opposite fear, that Christ will want to break through for me in the ways His supremacy promises. The whole idea of intimate encounters with Him feels unpredictable, disruptive, uncomfortable, and, most of all, costly. What if, when He draws near, He exposes me for who I really am? What if He takes me where I've never gone before? I fear the potential success of His supremacy manifested in my life.

3. The fear that I CAN'T.

No matter how powerfully or prosperously Christ's supremacy may break through for me, I dread the level of obedience He will expect of me as a result. I'm apprehensive that the action steps this will require of me will go beyond my ability to please Him. I fear the potential demands His supremacy will make of my life because I feel impotent to respond as fully as my King deserves.

There's good news for all who struggle with such fears. Grace can effectively challenge every "crisis of supremacy" (exhibited in part by each fear above) as the Spirit unveils more of the truth in Jesus. We rise with renewed expectations and holy ambitions toward our King. The Spirit can convince us that every promise of Jesus' reign will be accomplished without fail, that every demonstration of His reign will apply only God's best to us, and that every demand of His reign will be underwritten by His power and resources.

The Father wants us to revel daily in the preeminence of His Son. He invites us to do so right now in ways reflective of how we will celebrate Him in the blaze of His eternal dominion. In light of a full expectation of that final moment, He urges us in this present moment to abandon ourselves wholeheartedly to obedience to Christ.

In the day of glory all believers will prostrate themselves before the throne, not from terror but out of sheer unbounded adoration for the Lamb. We will be filled forever with unfettered fervency for His magnificent supremacy (Rev. 5). In greater measure than we have yet known, that experience can become much more ours even today.

QUOTABLE QUOTE

O, My God! In all my dangers, temporal and spiritual, I will hope in thee who art Almighty power, and therefore able to relieve me; who art infinite goodness and therefore ready and willing to assist me.

O, precious blood of my Redeemer,
O, gaping wounds of my crucified Savior.
Who can contemplate the sufferings of God incarnate, and not raise his hope, and not put his trust in Him?

Blessed hope! Be thou my chief delight in life, and then I shall be steadfast and immovable, always abounding in the work of the Lord.

("A PRAYER FOR HOPE"
BY RICHARD ALLEN — C. 1815)

Hopeful Repentance

Sometimes our joy in Jesus is suffocated by a self-absorbed arrogance that smugly assumes we have Him pretty well figured out already and don't need to know that much more. However, if we're ever to "abound in hope by the power of the Holy Spirit" (Rom. 15:13), God may need to recapture us for Christ's supremacy by leading us into repentance.

As one pastor put it, repentance is motivated by "an awakened taste for pleasure in God." We take at face value what Scripture says about where God is headed in His Son. We desire to head in that same direction with Him. So we eliminate everything that might get in the way, laying aside every sin that could entangle us or distract us as we run toward Christ alone (Heb. 12). We renounce anything within us that hinders the promotion of God's glorious purposes in Christ.

When was the last time we repented for what we have done to and against our Lord Jesus? Would you be willing to join me in these solemn confessions to the Father?

- We repent for how we have diminished Your Son, regarding Him more as our mascot than our Monarch.

- We repent for how we have manipulated Your Son, coming to Him to use Him, as far as we think we need Him—that far and no more.

- We repent for how we have hoarded Your Son, seeking His

blessings for ourselves, with little thought about bringing those blessings to others. We've assumed that He was there only for us. We've acted as if He was not Lord of neighbors and nations.

• We repent for how we have resisted Your Son, withholding our affections from Him because we were afraid of what it would cost us to draw near to Him; and thus we denied His lordship over all.

• We repent for how we've replaced Your Son with creeds, programs, organizations, and causes performed in His name but without the consuming passion He deserves as the Center and Circumference of everything for us and all peoples everywhere.

Dismantling

Another form of repentance also enlarges our capacity for a greater vision of God's Son—"dismantling," the laying aside of good things. These might include personal spiritual ambitions or commendable ministry projects—wonderful initiatives we may treasure for Jesus' sake but which, to our surprise, have begun to interfere with a sharper focus on His lordship. We may need to "dismantle"—to strip down, to repent of—dreams, activities, relationships, and priorities that were useful once to the Kingdom but are now hindering full enthusiasm for Christ's glory.

Maybe it is a worship style. Maybe it is a hobby. Maybe it is being too focused on the stock market or television. No matter how well intended or Christ centered in its appearance, if something in your life is

> **QUOTABLE QUOTE**
>
> *Surely Christ beckons us to repent of hearts that see Him so small that we think our works enrich Him, our programs support Him, our lives are indispensable to His plan. To see Him move and work in power for His name's sake must become our consuming passion, deepening and intensifying as His Spirit takes control of our hearts. Let us settle for nothing less than the explosive inhabitation of the living Lord.*
>
> (TRICIA RHODES)

not compatible with magnifying Jesus' majesty and extending His monarchy, it must be dismantled with impunity. You will grow in captivity to Christ's glory by dismantling even the good (when necessary) to be ready to receive more of God's best.

Reflection

Maybe it would be helpful for you to pause right here to reflect on a few questions most of us have never been asked before. They might help pinpoint where your passion for Christ needs to grow stronger in order to confront and cure the crisis of supremacy in your life.

1. What usually absorbs my affections on a daily basis? What genuinely preoccupies me?
2. What challenges arouse my interest? What causes inspire my commitment? Where do my true ambitions lie?
3. What do I consider to be the pinnacle of my life purpose, the reason I was created and redeemed in the first place?
4. In what ways has a vision of the glory of God's Son and the hope this guarantees ignited in me fervency for His supremacy?
5. How has the Father's passion for His Son stirred up my own desire to love Christ so much more?
6. Do I ever fear being labeled as one who has become too fanatical about Jesus or too radical for Him? Why is that? What do I really fear?
7. Am I prepared like Paul to pour out my life for an awakening in the church to Jesus for all He is? How will I confront the crisis of supremacy in my life or my church so that Jesus might receive the greater praise He deserves? What might this cost me?

Doxology and Challenge

Are you prepared to join me in declaring these words to Triune God?

> *We press into Your heart this day, glorious God and Father*
> *of our Lord Jesus Christ.*
> *We celebrate all that Your precious Son is—*
> *who He is to us, for us, over us, within us,*
> *through us, before us, and upon us.*

Before all heaven we proclaim:

- Christ is supreme! He is sovereign, superior, sufficient, and totally satisfying!
- Christ is our hope! He is the summation of all Your promises, the source of all Your riches, more and more and more, for now and forever!
- Christ is our glory! He is Alpha and Omega, the consummation of all Your purposes, for all creation, for all peoples, for all the ages to come! In Him our life is hidden with You until the hour He returns in the final triumphs of grace and truth.
- Christ is among us! He is accessible to us now, in all of His riches. He stands with us now, willing, able, and ready to act for us, in us, and through us to magnify ALL He is, before us and before all nations!

In light of the pervasive loss of hope in the Church, fostered by a crisis of supremacy on the *inside,* how might the church be flooded again with the Bible's magnificent message about the full extent of Christ's supremacy? What do you think you should do about it? Why should any serious Christian make His supremacy her or his premiere proclamation *to other Christians?*

Has the hour finally come for us seriously to consider a Campaign of Hope throughout the Church, one that is bent on restoring to believers a fresh vision of hope in God's Son for ALL He is? Can there be any more strategic step for any of us to undertake than a mission to awaken God's people to our glorious destiny in Jesus? If we do so, might they not join us in taking this same vision to neighbors and nations?

If this seems right, what could it mean for your own sense of mission for Christ?

GO DEEPER: Read Galatians 1:3-9; 3:1-5; 4:19; 6:14-18. Explore chapters 7 and 8 at *www.ReadCIA.com*.

NINETEEN

Why do Christians need to be reawakened to a larger hope in Christ?

A vision for transformation with biblical proportions invigorated the early days of the Civil Rights movement in America. In the midst of battling to secure prophetic justice for his people in the early 1960s, Rev. Martin Luther King reminded fellow believers (and all of us with them): "At times, we must accept finite disappointments. But we must never lose the infinite hope God gives us in Jesus!"

Instinctively every human being knows hope is what both individuals and civilizations need to survive and flourish. In the same sense hope is the key to the vitality and impact of Christians in any generation.

However, if not grounded in a comprehensive vision of Christ— if not shaped by everything He is, seated on His throne—every promising outlook we profess can quickly dissolve into uninvited crises of hope. Our one reliable refuge against every onslaught of hopelessness and despair is our bedrock conviction about the inexhaustible riches of His supremacy (Eph. 3).

But there's also good news each time hope is shaken. The experience can bring a blessing if the setback drives Christians to reexamine what we really believe about the glory of God's Son— and if in turn this wakes us up to all the hope we are meant to have because Jesus is Lord.

Hope and Human Survival

Without hope one can lapse into everything from lethargy to bitterness to mind-numbing gloom. We all need something to look forward to, something that holds promise of more than we have yet experienced.

> ## QUOTABLE QUOTE
>
> *One of the most fascinating of all the preacher's tasks is to explore both the emptiness of fallen man and the fullness of Jesus Christ in order then to demonstrate how He can fill our emptiness, lighten our darkness, enrich our poverty and bring our human aspirations to fulfillment. To encounter Christ is to touch reality and experience transcendence.*
>
> (Dr. John R. Stott)

Thoreau wrote that humans "live lives of quiet desperation" where hints of happy expectations quickly fade. Agnostic philosopher Bertrand Russell cynically concluded shortly before his death: "There is a darkness without. And when I die there will be darkness within. There is no splendor, no vastness anywhere, only triviality for a moment, and then nothing." Jean-Paul Sarte confessed the same despair: "I've discovered I'm alive, and the thought of it sickens me." How many of us at one time or another hear ourselves asking: "Is this all there is to life? Is this as good as it will get?"

By comparison Viktor Frankl, who studied Jewish prisoners in German concentration camps, wrote *A Man's Search for Meaning*. In it he documents the resilient power of "hope-fullness." What made the difference between those who survived and those who perished, he found, was often the degree of hope they nourished. Those who prevailed through horrible trials did so primarily because they were convinced there was "something beyond the barbed wire to live for, something to look forward to, something to go home to."

Roots of Hopelessness

Above every other explanation, the Bible is clear that humankind is deprived of lasting hope simply because we are dead in sin and dead to God (Eph. 2). Psalm 7:14 (NIV) notes that "he who is pregnant with evil and conceives trouble gives birth to disillusionment," to shattered dreams. And yet the nature of sin is often to keep us defiant, seeking self-made solutions with an arrogance that God critiques like this: "You were tired out by the length of your road, yet you did not say, 'It is hopeless'" (Isa. 57:10).

False fulfillments embedded in alluring Western materialism have left many people ambivalent. Not a few have found that a sense of superabundance fostered unanticipated fear—fear over how material blessings of such a magnitude simply could not last much longer.

On the flip side, multitudes of others have succumbed to hopelessness in the midst of want—poverty, misfortune, disease, violence, and oppression. An estimated 40 million poor residing in the U.S. alone, many of whom are also our brothers and sisters in Christ, have been stripped of dignity and diminished by demons of doom day after day.

Our world is being slashed to pieces by waves of injustice, brutality, terrorism, poverty, racism, phantom affluence, perversion, and epidemics. How do we convince people imprisoned in a canyon full of broken dreams to risk believing that some form of concrete, lasting hope still exists?

Hopelessness and the Heart

When you get right down to it, every modern expression of insufficient hope—whether for believers or unbelievers—hits at the heart level. Gordon MacDonald reminds us that even Christians can lose personal hope due to the basic heartaches of life, such as when:

- marriages go sour.
- investments go "south."
- catastrophic illnesses overtake us.

- youthful ambitions hit the wall of midlife limitations.
- someone we deeply love dies.
- our own mortality threatens us.

Such setbacks can crush any of us, challenging at the core what we say we believe about Christ's supremacy.

On top of this, Jesus' followers frequently find themselves taunted with additional misgivings uniquely experienced by saints, troubling questions pagans would never even think to ask. For starters, in the midst of every difficult challenge the world faces, Christians must come back to foundational issues of faith, such as: Does God's Word promise tangible triumphs through His Son that I can anticipate at this moment with confidence? Is He actively shaping my future right now or just watching it unfold?

Now I ask you: What Muslim, Hindu, or hedonist do you know who feels it necessary to address at this level such personal questions about hopefulness?

Magnitude of the Task

A major reason for loss of hope relates to the task God has given us. Many are disabled with hopelessness because of their erroneous perception that U.S. and world evangelization has failed. Numbers of believers are unsettled over what seems like disturbing discrepancies between what the Church claims about the outcome of Christ's mission to the world and what has actually been accomplished so far. Equally, they are stymied by the magnitude of what remains to be done.

For example, in the U.S. urban challenges can seem too formidable for the gospel to handle. Poor housing, injustice, addictions, and crime appear virtually unstoppable. Many Christians conclude incorrectly that few tangible evidences exist where the lordship of Jesus effectively turned the tide. Cut-and-run becomes much easier as we say to one another, "Let's just try to hold the fort until Jesus comes back again!"

After 2,000 years of massive, sacrificial efforts, why does it seem we still have so far to go? Despite bold beginnings in the book of Acts, why have 67 percent of all humans from A.D. 30 to the present day never heard the name of Jesus (as documented by the *World Christian Encyclopedia*)? Quite honestly, it is hard to sustain hope in Christ and His supremacy for personal challenges when we conclude that the immensity of the larger mission is still too elusive.

Disappointed with Christ

The most disabling form of despair any Christian can experience is this: our personal, secret disappointments with Christ Himself.

Frankly this tragedy is more prevalent in our churches than most care to confess. Many have concluded privately that they will never consistently experience what the Bible says an abundant life in Christ looks like. They've not been transformed into genuine Christlikeness. The victorious Christian life has not unfolded the way they thought it was supposed to, and they're deeply confounded.

Unmet longings for promised spiritual advances suggest that Christ somehow has failed us. He has not brought to pass what we have every right to expect from Someone who declares utterly to love us while at the same time holding sway over an entire creation. If truth were told, you and I have probably backlogged scores of

> ## QUOTABLE QUOTE
>
> *Very few American Christians have experienced a sense of spiritual brokenness that compelled them to beg God for His mercy and acceptance through the love of Christ.*
> *We have a nation of "Christians" who took the best offer, but relatively few who were so humiliated and hopeless before a holy and omnipotent God that they cried out for undeserved compassion.*
> *That helps to explain why in practical terms it's hard to tell the difference between those who have beliefs that characterize them as born again and those who don't.*
>
> (DR. GEORGE BARNA)

prayers for help and healing that inexplicably still remain unanswered.

As psychologist John Eldredge reminds us, such doubts can unleash "the most poisonous" lies in Satan's arsenal. Using them to intensify every other form of hopelessness, the Tempter whispers: "For you personally, things will never, ever change!"

If what I've described feels familiar, remember you are not alone. Take a look at the smiling saints around you politely perched in their pews while singing God's praises on a Sunday morning. Scores harbor secret sorrows just as you may.

With reticence we wonder if we'll ever know consistency in how God fulfills the possibilities proclaimed from the pulpit. In the words of Brennan Manning, loss of confidence in the overarching dominion of God's Son causes "incalculable harm to Christian spirituality," leaving in its wake "the flotsam of distrustful, cynical Christians, angry at a capricious God." We just never say so aloud.

It's regrettable that no forum exists in most churches today where Christians may openly confess their disillusions. We have no place to debrief the soul's pain, no safe haven to explore troubled hearts, no mutually supportive ways to dismantle crises of hope. Instead many practice what Dallas Willard calls a "conspiracy of silence" by covering up the ways our lives contradict the claims of biblical promises.

Things deteriorate further as we stand aloof from signs of new beginnings. We're alarmed whenever God appears to be urging us to trust His Son "just one more time" for prospects that seem either

> ## QUOTABLE QUOTE
>
> *All of us need to be aware of how Christ is moving in the midst of His Church toward the end of all things, and equally aware of our deep and immediate intimacy with Him. The one who dwells in the midst of His church is bringing closure to our present age. We cannot help but have a strong sense of living at the edge of the final consummation. We breathe the very air of the impending Kingdom.*
>
> (DONALD MOSTROM)

110

too good to be true or have appeared elusive in the past. We tremble at the thought that if renewed reliance on Christ evaporates it may permanently shatter our ability to trust Him for anything enduring.

Christians who lose hopeful hearts develop spiritual paralysis. When part of a person's physical body is paralyzed, that individual may have commendable ambitions but often to little avail. The common frustration of paralytics is that they feel trapped by an inability to do with their bodies what their minds can visualize and what their hearts desire.

Reduced to spiritual paralytics, we may dream big dreams of what we'd like to do for the glory of Christ. But little, personally or corporately, seems to cooperate. Grappling with the same disheartening challenges our unbelieving neighbors experience, we pull back from the clear light of Scripture's teaching on the reign of Christ.

The implications of this are huge. Any loss of hope inside the church wounds our witness outside the church. It guts the credibility of our claims to a deeper spirituality. It significantly paralyzes our mission to neighbors and nations. It reveals to the world that our vision of God's Son is too small. In turn, our message about the Kingdom unravels into little more than meaningless mutterings.

Reason for Great Hope

More than a few Christians *have* prevailed in the battle, however. For many the crisis of supremacy has been substantially confronted and cured. In light of what we just discussed above, it is no small thing that millions of them are exhibiting this fresh "awakening to Christ" and are praying for fellow believers to be reawakened at the same time.

Thankfully, despair does not hold the final word for believers in America (or anywhere else). The final word—about history, humanity, destiny, eternity, mystery—belongs to God's Son. Our message of hope must begin and end by pointing to Him as the One to see, seek, and speak about for ALL He is.

Without question America is fertile ground for a movement toward the recovery of hope. The Church is primed for a major campaign to help spread biblical hope everywhere, first of all by confronting and curing the crisis of supremacy inside the Church. As the next seven chapters will make clear, an awakening to Christ and to hope not only is possible but probable.

GO DEEPER: Read Psalms 20; 24; 68. Explore chapters 1 and 6 at *www.ReadCIA.com*.

TWENTY

What is a Christ Awakening anyway?

The church in many parts of the world, but especially in America, desperately needs a God-given, Christ Awakening movement. That's what any genuine Campaign of Hope fosters and serves. Kingdom-shaped hope is always the first evidence of, as well as the premiere blessing from, a reawakening among God's people to the supremacy of God's Son. Biblical hope is more than a verb (as in "I hope so"). Biblical hope is ultimately a person (as in "My hope is in the LORD").

Christ is the source of profound approximations of that hope poured out on His Church every day in a host of ways. Among those blessings is one we sometimes call a "spiritual awakening," or even more clear, a Christ Awakening. Whether with an individual, a congregation, or a whole nation, every God-initiated revival—every Christ Awakening—is a foretaste of the "final revival," the one awaiting us at the moment Christ openly returns as reigning King of kings.

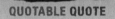

QUOTABLE QUOTE

Preach Christ, always and everywhere. He is the whole Gospel. His person, His offices and work must be our one great, all-comprehending theme.

(CHARLES SPURGEON)

Current missionary-sending endeavors from Asian, African, and Latin American churches may be the greatest confirmation yet of the impact of Christ-saturated vision among God's people. From these churches, however, thousands of laborers are being sent out by believers who in many cases live in abject poverty. Yet an awakened confidence in the supremacy of God's Son compels them to take risks for advancing the gospel that most Christians in the West know nothing about. Many have told me personally they do so with an unhesitant conviction that, in the words of Habakkuk 2:14, the nations will soon "be filled with the knowledge of the glory of the LORD, as the waters cover the sea."

One Christian's View

One of history's most perceptive writers on the topic of revival was Jonathan Edwards. A brilliant New England pastor/scholar during the early to mid 1700s, Edwards argued that revival held a central place in the purposes of God.

Here's how he reasoned: God's objective in creation is to prepare a Kingdom for His Son. All of God's activities are moving unhesitatingly toward the Consummation of all things. Based on that nonnegotiable, Edwards concluded, the revival of God's people must comprise one of Christ's most strategic activities between His Ascension and return.

Fortunately Edwards had the privilege of observing revival firsthand across his own New England and eventually in his own congregation. Scholars call the phenomenon "the First Great Awakening."

In New Testament-style revival Christians are aroused to a reality of Christ's presence and power already theirs but currently overlooked. They are summoned not only to recapture their first love for Him (Rev. 2) but also to discover a passion for Him that surpasses whatever they have known before (Eph. 3).

That's why, as Edwards observed, revival is arguably the most dramatic display of Jesus' lordship in

> ### QUOTABLE QUOTE
>
> *We ought to read the Scriptures with the express design of finding Christ in them. Whoever shall turn aside from this object, though he may weary himself throughout his whole life in learning, will never attain the knowledge of the truth: for what wisdom can we have without the wisdom of God?*
>
> (JOHN CALVIN)

114

the present age. In no way depreciating God's ordinary work with us on a daily basis, these exceptional seasons of His *extraordinary* work accelerate every other foretaste of the age to come.

Past Awakenings

Following each one of the four so-called great awakenings in American history (early 1700s, late 1700s, mid 1800s, early 1900s), decades of documented transformations took place both in churches and in society. God gave His people "fresh winds," not simply to fire up enthusiasm for spiritual things but also to extend further the reign of His Son within communities and nations through His church.

At the close of the twentieth century, a wonderful move of God also came to the beleaguered nation of Uganda. Once known as the "jewel of Africa," this beautiful land had become devastated, physically and spiritually, by multiple oppressive regimes headed by diabolical dictators. Tens of thousands of Christians were martyred for their faith, many by unspeakable tortures.

As a result, hundreds of thousands began to cry out to God for a spiritual awakening in their land. The believers grappled with the need for soul-searching repentance inside the church. They confessed all the ways they were actually complicit in His judgments on Uganda as a whole. Broken in spirit, they pled for God's mercy rather than prosperity or safety.

> **QUOTABLE QUOTE**
>
> *Here we are in the North American church cranking along just fine, thank you...managing the machinery, utilizing biblical principles, celebrating recovery, user-friendly, techno savvy...growing in self-esteem, reinventing ourselves as effective ecclesiastical entrepreneurs, and, in general, feeling ever so much better about our achievements. Notice anything missing in this pretty picture? JESUS CHRIST!*
>
> (BISHOP WILLIAM WILLIMON)

Finally God answered their cries. Joyous confidence about Christ's Kingdom reignited their churches. Passion for the Promise Giver once again marked thousands of congregations large and small. But this was just the beginning of revival.

At the same time ungodly strongmen were unexpectedly expelled. Corrupt structures of oppression were decisively dismantled. Political and religious prisoners were set free. Persecution of the church came to an end. A devoutly righteous Christian leader became Uganda's president. He made his first official act a public rededication of the entire nation to Jesus Christ as its Lord!

Following that, to the amazement of all, significant economic recovery began. Far more importantly, in Uganda (once known as the African nation with the largest AIDS epidemic) a nationwide commitment to sexual abstinence turned back the plague—all in just one decade! Some of the largest churches in Africa are now found there, with one in Kampala growing from a few hundred to nearly 15,000 in five years. Fasting and prayer became a way of life for Ugandan Christians as they sought even deeper manifestations of Christ's reign in their generation.

Stories like this are multiplying everywhere. A half decade into the twenty-first century, one of Latin America's leading evangelists, addressing an all-night prayer vigil of 250,000 in Mexico City, declared: "Latin America is at the threshold of an enormous spiritual awakening!" The Argentine-born Alberto Mottesi continued: "This will bring forth revival in the economic, political, and social arenas. It reminds me of what happened in Martin Luther's Reformation which became the preamble to the Renaissance, affecting the arts and culture. We are going to see something similar in Latin America."

> **QUOTABLE QUOTE**
>
> *The person of Jesus is our hope. Redeeming and transforming our nature, Jesus has taken it to heaven where he bears it now faithfully before his Father, in our name and on our behalf. Jesus ascended is himself the promise and the hope that we will share in that glory, now in part but one day in full.*
>
> (DR. GERRIT SCOTT DAWSON)

Surely these are the kinds of stories God is willing to compose for His Son within churches and communities everywhere. Call it revival, spiritual awakening, or a Christ Awakening. But call it, without a doubt, "approximations of the Consummation!"

Revival as "Arrival"

At the last day, in the final revival, the entire universe will be awakened fully to all that Christ is. It will be summoned into full participation in His unconditional lordship. In every other revival, though on a lesser scale, God still wants to pursue a recovery of more comprehensive visions of His Son among His people.

Steve Hawthorne suggests revival might, therefore, be called "arrival." It's as if Christ "shows up" in His church afresh to recapture us and reconquer us.

> ### QUOTABLE QUOTE
>
> *In Christ, the triumphant Messianic age arrived, (the age) that only God could establish, and only in Christ was it established. In Christ, we are face to face with God; before Christ we are in the presence of eternity.*
>
> (DR. DAVID WELLS)

The Puritans coined a great phrase to define the "arrival" experience. They called such seasons "the *manifest* presence of Christ." Here is how they reasoned. First, there is Christ's *essential* presence. That is, Christ is everywhere present all the time. He is unavoidable. Second, they also talked about Christ's *cultivated* presence. Christians can enrich their sense of fellowship with Him as they abide in Him day by day, faithfully obeying Him. We may cultivate a deeper knowledge of the Lord through Bible study and prayer. As we do, Christ shows Himself to be much more present in our lives than we had realized.

The *manifest* presence of Christ was something else altogether. This was the Puritans' third term for those times when God reveals His Son to a new generation of His people. He does so in such dramatic fashion that it almost seems as if Christ has been hiding from us until that moment. Then suddenly He reinserts Himself among us. He arrives. This encounter cannot be cultivated. It is a gift from the living God and must be received.

Until the Consummation our Redeemer intends to continue invading His church, extending His lordship among us, regaining the praise He rightfully deserves, and enlarging His mission through us among all earth's peoples. Revival is one of the most exciting expressions of Christ's supremacy any Christian can experience until He comes again.

All of which brings us back to our original definition of a Christ Awakening. It is ...

when God's Spirit uses God's Word
to reintroduce God's people to God's Son
for all He is.

GO DEEPER: Read Acts 19:1-20. Explore chapters 1, 11 and appendix VI at *www.ReadCIA.com*.

TWENTY-ONE

Are you ready to foster a Christ Awakening movement as a Messenger of Hope?

An amateur painter once tried to develop his own version of Leonardo da Vinci's *The Last Supper*. After giving it his best shot, he showed his efforts to a few friends. He was brokenhearted when one remarked: "My, what exquisite detail you have incorporated on the cups the disciples are holding!" Realizing he had failed to make Jesus the central focus of his painting as he had intended, he destroyed the canvas and started over.

Messengers of Hope are like painters. Our mission is to pass along life-changing portraits of Jesus that make Him the major focus for other believers. But how does one effectively deliver these portraits for maximum impact on God's people? Is there some tested and proven strategy that, combined with God's Word, effectively awakens believers to reform their pursuit of Jesus' glory?

Restore the Whole Vision

To revitalize the whole Church to take the whole gospel to the whole world, we must restore the *whole vision* of God's Son among God's people. We must strive to proclaim a message that almost "reconverts" Christians to Christ for ALL He is—for the completion of the Great Commission and the Consummation of the ages.

The crisis of supremacy is so intractable and so pervasive that it will never be cured with halfhearted measures. What is needed is a genuine, all-out campaign—a campaign for the glory of Christ, a campaign to restore hope and passion toward Christ, a campaign that involves each of us as Messengers of Hope. We must set about the task of delivering to fellow Christians a radically biblical Message of Hope. And we must do so without delay.

To have impact the campaign must spread far and wide. The message must be delivered by an ardent army of heralds inside the church. A Campaign of Hope must enlist Christians like you and me who care whether Christ receives the glory He deserves among His people. As Messengers of Hope we must proclaim a larger vision of the King throughout the body, holding nothing back as we do. In fact, that's precisely what this book envisions: a magnificent movement of messengers—a church flooded with Christ proclaimers!

The stakes are high, especially in our witness for Christ to neighbors and nations. Only as we carry out a Campaign of Hope successfully *inside* our churches will Christians be able and willing to embrace wholeheartedly our mission to earth's unreached peoples outside our churches (compare Isa. 60 with 1 Thess. 1).

> **QUOTABLE QUOTE**
>
> *From every text of Scripture there is a road to Christ. And my dear brother, your business is, when you get to a text, to say, now, what is the road to Christ? I have never found a text that did not have a road to Christ in it.*
>
> (CHARLES SPURGEON)

Nothing any of us could choose to do at this moment is more strategic, for the advance of the Kingdom of God's dear Son before the nations, than to promote a vision for the full extent of Christ's lordship among one another as believers. Each of us must begin right now to make a decisive difference in our churches by what we say about the Savior to disciples who sit with us every Sunday.

A Campaign of Hope

In some ways a Campaign of Hope could be similar to a political campaign. This campaign can recruit citizens in the Empire of the Son to reengage with Him—with His cause, His platform, His policies,

His promises, His credibility, and His administration—fanning into flame fresh fervor for His Royal Majesty.

Those involved in a Campaign of Hope will set out to convince fellow believers there is so much more—more that Christ deserves, more that He desires, more that He has designed, and more that He has decreed—and then get others praying and acting like it, filled with renewed anticipation! Hope is one of the most marvelous manifestations of Christ's reign for a Christian, congregation, or nation.

Be Encouraged

The potential for renewal is unparalleled. God's miracle-working grace already has preceded such a campaign. Already the Spirit has rekindled countless Christians waiting in the wings, hungry for a fresh message about the greatness of God's Son, eager to band with us to exalt Him in new ways. Already, God is raising up a multitude of willing proclaimers poised for action. I've met with thousands of them around the world the past two decades. And there are literally millions more.

These "change agents" must be mobilized as quickly as possible. Invite the Spirit to flow through you as you help them become captivated by hope, living out the promises Jesus secures for them. Then recruit them as Messengers of Hope themselves, equipped to present to fellow Christians a more dynamic vision of Jesus that calls them to be awakened to Him for ALL He is. Your equipping and then reproducing yourself through others comprises the Campaign of Hope I'm calling for.

I'm convinced a Campaign of Hope is already rising in today's church! And I pray that you, my reader, will eventually choose to become part of it (if you haven't already). Is the Holy Spirit calling you to move forward with such a campaign?

Are You Ready?

Considering all that hangs in the balance, you might want to take a moment right now to ask yourself:

1. Do I personally know Christ well enough to present Him to other Christians fully enough to help them come back to Him for all He is?

2. Do I know how to speak to other believers about a vision of Christ that's grand enough to start healing their disappointments from the past and delivering them from daunting fears about the future?

3. Am I so confident about Christ's total sufficiency for the heart cries of the human soul that I am willing to exalt Him to fellow Christians without apologies every chance I get?

4. And have I ever offered myself to the Father for this primary purpose: to be reawakened by His Spirit to the greater glory of His Son so I can effectively invite other Christians to recover hope in Christ's supremacy?

Describing a Messenger of Hope

I have pinpointed 13 characteristics evident in almost every Christ proclaimer I've met. No single messenger may exhibit all 13 at any one time. But most effective messengers in Scripture, as well as many from church history, displayed most of them. Numerous twenty-first-century Christians bear the same marks. The following can be reproduced in any believer by the power of the Spirit.

- *Single-Minded*—Messengers of Hope determine to make Christ and His supremacy their primary message.
- *Visionary*—Messengers of Hope help Christians interpret every facet of life from the perspective of Christ's all-encompassing reign.
- *Consistent*—Messengers of Hope give Christ daily obedience.
- *Prayerful*—Messengers of Hope pray that their messages will help reintroduce believers to Christ and His supremacy.
- *Compassionate*—Hope givers and Christ givers are also care-givers sent to Christians in the grip of despair and disillusionment to minister a fresh vision of Jesus' glory.

- *Reasonable*—By providing biblical rationales for living with abounding hope in God, Messengers of Hope seek to convince their hearers to make Christ their "all in all" (Col. 3).
- *Humble*—Christ proclaimers have no desire to promote themselves.
- *Foreteller*—Messengers of Hope challenge believers to anticipate approximations of the ultimate dominion of Christ by how He manifests His everlasting reign among them right now.
- *Forth-Teller*—They study and teach God's Word as a book of hope.
- *Decisive*—Exercising tough love, they challenge God's people to confront their own deficiencies in vision of Jesus and His Kingdom.
- *Mobilizer*—Messengers of Hope are proactive and move out to flood the Church with Campaigns of Hope.
- *Expectant*—Messengers of Hope are confident of the ultimate outcome of their efforts.
- *Coproclaimer*—Throughout their mission messengers never lose sight of how Christ actually preaches through them (2 Cor. 13), right in the midst of the congregation (Heb. 2), so that in every proclamation of God's promises not one voice is heard but rather two.

How many of these characteristics do you find at the forefront of your service to Christ already? Where do you want to grow?

Four Responses

In a parable about four different soils, Jesus illustrated four possible responses to His "word of the Kingdom" (Matt. 13:19). You will find it prudent to be ready for similar outcomes.

> ### QUOTABLE QUOTE
>
> *Whatever God has promised gets stamped with the Yes of Jesus. In him, this is what we preach and pray, the great Amen, God's Yes and our Yes together, gloriously evident. God affirms us, making us a sure thing in Christ, putting his Yes within us.*
>
> (2 CORINTHIANS 1:20-21 – THE MESSAGE)

When fellow believers hear you, some will appear hardhearted. Others will turn weak hearted. Still others will respond with half-hearted measures. This will disappoint you deeply. But by God's grace some will choose to be wholehearted! They will grab hold of your Message of Hope with great expectations and determine to live in the light of its Kingdom promises. As it was for Jesus, so it will be for you: wholehearted disciples must remain our primary audience in any Campaign of Hope. Be on the lookout for them.

> ### QUOTABLE QUOTE
>
> *Anyone who reads even a smattering of Paul's writing recognizes early on that his devotion to Christ was the foremost reality and passion of his life. "For me to live is Christ; to die is to gain Christ." Christ is the beginning and goal of everything for Paul, and thus is the single great reality along the way.*
>
> (DR. GORDON FEE)

Regarding the other three soils, however, let me encourage you: before your message about Jesus' glorious greatness was shared with them, most were locked up in boxes of shrunken vision, feeble faith, and dead-end prospects. Now you have them wondering if a truly fulfilling life, a life lived in the wide-open spaces of Jesus' forcefully advancing Kingdom, might possibly happen for them.

Do you recall the last time you raised spiritual issues with some of God's people? Maybe it was during a luncheon Bible study at the office, in a conversation with a friend between church services, or during deliberations at the last missions committee meeting. Maybe it was last night at family devotions or while visiting a friend in the hospital. Ask yourself:

1. The last time I shared God's Word from my heart with other believers, did I unfold for them a larger vision of Christ and His supremacy than what they had before we met?

2. At the same time, did I lay out for them more compelling reasons to put their hope in Christ, and to do so with greater confidence, than what they had before we met?

For a Messenger of Hope, saying yes to such questions is the sign of success, as God measures success. We have succeeded anytime people can say, "Through what you shared with me you opened up for me a larger vision of Christ's grace and glory than I had ever seen before! And now my hope in Him and my passion for Him are stronger than ever."

Gathering with Others

Once you've uncovered a few other Christ-enthused believers who are willing to work together for a Christ Awakening movement, consider meeting together. You may wonder what to do whenever you come together. Here are a few ideas. They can be used with a new group you create, or they can be incorporated into an existing small group that is waking up to Christ:

1. Above all, talk about Christ. In what ways has your vision of Christ expanded since you were last together?
2. Share the hope that is already growing in your own hearts. Talk about what you anticipate God will do in your life (as well as in the world) in the days to come.
3. Talk about what you see God doing among others even now.
4. Talk honestly about your struggles, disappointments, sufferings, doubts, and fears.
5. Report on ways you are seeking to stir up hope in other believers.
6. Focus on building into one another fresh confidence toward God.
7. Study specific Scripture passages on hope and the supremacy of God's Son.
8. Discuss what practical changes each of you need to make in light of the insights into Christ you've just uncovered.
9. Spend much time praying together.

10. End each session by recommissioning one another to herald this wonderful vision of Christ's supremacy to everyone you meet and to bring others with you into all the hope Christians were meant to have.

We magnify God's Son to one another because we know faith comes by hearing, when what gets heard is the message of Christ (Rom. 10:17). As disciples grow to appreciate greater dimensions of His lordship, He will reveal Himself increasingly to us in ways comparable to His person and power.

When God gives such a result, we've effectively launched out into the one mission that really matters. We have taken a strategic step toward confronting and curing the crisis of supremacy as we foster and serve the movement right where we live.

GO DEEPER: Read Acts 11:20-27; 13:1-3; 14:23-28. Explore chapters 9 and 10 at *www.ReadCIA.com*.

TWENTY-TWO

How can prayer set the stage for a Christ Awakening?

Citizens of Pasadena, California, are grateful when the winds blow the suffocating smog from the San Gabriel Valley out to sea. As a result, they enjoy a view of the magnificent San Gabriel Mountains, previously veiled for days by brownish haze. The view puts a bounce in their steps and a song in their hearts.

In the same way the Holy Spirit, God's wholesome wind of hope, desires to fill every believer. The Spirit wants to provide clear vistas on our Victorious Redeemer, removing all foggy thinking about Him and enlarging our horizons of hope as we breathe in the freshness of His Kingdom promises. When that happens, prayer is never far behind.

Prayer and Hope in Christ

Prayerfulness and hopefulness are inseparably linked. First, God gives us a vision for the future that is so wonderful we conclude we cannot live without it. But then He helps us realize it is so wonderful we cannot personally produce it. Can't live without it; can't produce it? That's when our primary option becomes to seek it—to pray for it. We are compelled to ask the Father to accomplish for us the hope we long for and the promises we are so helpless to produce by ourselves.

That's what makes prayer such a dependable barometer of what's happening with hope inside any congregation. An absence of prayer in church priorities should ring an alarm. The pall of hopelessness may be hanging over us more than we thought. Fears of defeat fasten onto a people clutched by the crisis of supremacy.

The good news is that we don't have to remain stuck in these waterless pits. If I've learned anything over the past 30 years of working with prayer leaders and prayer movements all over the world, it is this:

> The single most important ingredient
> for igniting and sustaining a united work of prayer
> is simply to clarify for everyone, at every opportunity,
> the hope that Christ's supremacy calls us to pray *toward*.

That's why Messengers of Hope inside a congregation will usually double as mobilizers of prayer. Prayer becomes the necessary response of anyone who seriously heeds a message of the hope the supremacy of Christ is for us.

Movements of Prayer

Recent research indicates that nearly 200 million Christians worldwide are committed to praying for the advancement of Christ's Kingdom as a daily spiritual discipline. Over 40 million of these meet to do so in small weekly prayer groups. In other words, already many are waking up enough to our magnificent hope in Christ to set themselves in the pursuit of His purposes with determined desire for God to work.

Stepping from the throne room into living rooms, they will be able to speak authentically to believers about a grander vision of Jesus because that vision drove them to prayer in the first place. Hundreds of praying Christians are already making this transition.

Throughout history, concerted prayer movements have provided launching pads for major advances of Christ's Kingdom. This was certainly true with four major religious awakenings in our nation the past two centuries. As God's people kept praying, each awakening overflowed into revitalized churches and denominations, significant social reforms, widespread evangelistic ingatherings, and the creation of scores of new mission-sending societies.

Today the scope and urgency of prayers going up from literally millions of saints in many nations is committed to a similar awakening to the glory of God's Son. The historical pattern should forewarn us: Get ready! Extraordinary new displays of Christ's dominion are on their way!

Four Dimensions of Prayer

When Messengers of Hope pray, they lay hold onto four concerns to shape their praises and prayers before the throne. Put simply:

> ## QUOTABLE QUOTE
>
> *The early church believed Jesus Christ to be divine. It applied to him the highest conceivable designations (Son of God, Son of Man, Lord, God); it saw him as possessing the full range of divine attributes, performing the full range of divine functions and enjoying the full range of divine prerogatives; it worshipped him and prayed to him and broke out in doxology at the mere mention of his name. These early Christians did not simply catch the faith of Jesus; they had faith in Jesus.*
>
> (Dr. Donald MacLeod)

1. Many of God's promises encourage us to seek Him for a fresh *focus* on Christ Himself that we might know Him better for ALL He is. Our prayers must seize on this grand prospect, asking the Father to reveal more of His Son's glory to us, our churches, and the nations.

2. Other passages reassure us that God intends to grant greater *fulfillments* of Christ's mission—in evangelism, justice, healing, church planting, feeding the hungry, etc.

3. A host of other promises invite us to pray for fresh experiences of Christ's *fullness* in our lives and in our churches as He lives out

His reign among us—including Christ's gifts for ministry (1 Cor. 12), the fruit of His Spirit (Gal. 5), His wisdom and counsel (Eph. 1), and His empowerment for outreach (Acts 1).

4. Other texts compel intercession for renewed *fervency*. We ask the Father to ignite within us deeper devotion for His Son, to strengthen us by His Spirit to live for Jesus, and to impact others through all the gifts and resources He has given us.

Every biblically based prayer a Christian expresses incorporates one or more of these primary dimensions of Christ's supremacy. In similar fashion we may expect every answer to our prayers to advance Christ's glory in one or more of these same four dimensions.

Six Responses

On top of the four dimensions of prayer, Messengers of Hope should also incorporate the six major biblical responses of prayer.

1. REJOICE means that you:
   - Praise the Father as the God who is, who was, and who is to come—the God of all hope.
   - Rejoice in the prospects of greater glory for Christ ahead, both in this world and in the world to come.
   - Thank Him for so many promises already fulfilled in the past.
   - Celebrate how He will bring greater honor to His Son as He accomplishes His purposes in the church and among the nations.

> ### QUOTABLE QUOTE
>
> *The arrival of Christ in heaven changed the character of heaven forever. This was the first time perfect humanity entered the presence of God. He was the first man in heaven with a resurrected body. Never before had there been a man with nail prints at the center of the universe. (Now) He fills all things by His presence, His sovereignty, His activity.*
>
> (DR. ERWIN LUTZER)

- Above all, proclaim in prayer all that Christ means to you—who He is to you, for you, over you, within you, through you, before you, and upon you.

2. REPENT means that you:

- Make specific confession of both the individual and corporate sins that quench your passion for Christ's glory, diminish your spirit of hope in Him, hinder your enthusiasm for His Kingdom, or diminish your joy over the Consummation itself (the final display of His lordship).
- Declare your willingness to turn away from everything that might hinder the full realization of God's promises in your life in Christ.
- Make similar confession over the besetting sins of your nation.
- Acknowledge how your sins, relationships, ambitions, even Christian traditions, may hinder the outworking of God's promises by quenching, grieving, and resisting the Holy Spirit.
- Plead for God's mercy for all His people because we have diminished, distorted, and dishonored Christ for who He really is.

3. RESIST means that you:

- Intercede over every situation where you sense the Enemy seeks to thwart the unfolding of God's promises.
- Pray for thorough victories over Satan's strategies against advances of Christ's kingdom.
- Combat strongholds raised up against the vision of Christ and His supremacy, both inside and outside the church.
- Resist Satan's efforts to rob us of hope and distract us from the Consummation as well as from approximations of it now.

4. REQUEST means that you:

- Offer bold prayers for the promises of God to be fulfilled in greater measure. Apply specific promises to specific situations.

- Intercede for the supremacy of Christ to be more clearly revealed in your life, your church, your community, your nation, and the world.
- Seek God's outpouring of refreshing encounters with any and all four dimensions of God's promises: focus, fulfillment, fullness, and fervency.
- Plead for a powerful increase in the worldwide missionary endeavor.
- Intercede for the return of Christ in glory!

5. RECEIVE means that you:

- Pinpoint periods of silence simply to listen to what God may want to say back to you as you pray. Prayer is a two-way conversation!
- Expect Him also to reinforce your hope about what you've already prayed by increasing your confidence in what the future holds as the answers come.
- Receive fresh clarifications from the Holy Spirit for your daily discipleship and ministry so that everything you do will be conducted in anticipation of more to come.
- Above all, look for your passion for Christ to be fanned aflame as you listen while waiting to receive His responses to your prayers.

6. RECOMMIT means that you:

- Offer yourself anew to the Lord Jesus Christ in view of the promises you have just prayed about.
- Express readiness to be involved in the answers to your prayers, no matter what it may cost.
- Seek the Spirit's (re)filling to empower you for everything that ongoing anticipatory discipleship may demand of you.
- Above all, surrender to the Spirit to reignite your passion for Christ alone and for the great hope you have in Him.

Three Answers to Prayer

Immediate Answers—Because all answered prayer results in decisive demonstrations of Christ's dominion to someone, somewhere, it should come as no surprise that God begins to grant that ultimate answer to His praying children in more immediate ways the moment we begin to seek Him. When we draw near, He draws near (James 4). Christ meets us personally in prayer even when wider, more tangible outworkings of our requests don't seem to occur, at least in our timetable. He gives us intimacy with Himself in His supremacy in direct relationship to why we're praying in His name in the first place.

Intermediate Answers—Heaven's initial breakthroughs, even if they are not yet all we are longing for, are evidences of God at work for the intercessors. He is giving down payments on the age to come. Miracles, healings, financial supplies, restored relationships, opened doors for ministry, relief for the poor, victories over besetting sins—we must be vigilant so we don't miss any such intermediate answers. Jesus reigns; He always is active.

Consummate Answers—Every Christ-exalted, biblically grounded prayer we have ever prayed will be thoroughly answered. It will happen on the day Christ returns. Whether prayers for justice, defeat of dark powers, racial reconciliation, unity in the church, revival, or unreached peoples, all will be consummated in a manner exceedingly beyond what we might dare to imagine today (Eph. 3).

> ## QUOTABLE QUOTE
>
> *At the beginning God expressed himself. That personal expression, that word, was with God, and was God, and he existed with God from the beginning. All creation took place through him and none took place without him. In him appeared life and this life was the light of mankind. The light still shines in the darkness and the darkness has never put it out.... So the Word of God became a human being and lived among us.*
>
> (JOHN 1:1-5, 14 – PHILLIPS TRANSLATION)

Furthermore, when the Consummation dawns, we will discover to our great joy that our work of intercession became one of God's chief means to reach that wonderful end. Plain and simple, all prayer is about extending the supremacy of Christ from here to eternity.

Therefore, all prayers to the Father about the Kingdom can be distilled into one word: *Come!* And all answers boil down to one person: *Christ!*

God has ordained the end. He also has ordained the means to that end. And chief among those means is the powerful impact of our prayers.

Come, Lord Jesus!
Come, ultimately, in the triumphs of Your victorious return.
But until then come with similarly transforming power
even now, right where we live.
Pour out preliminary experiences of Your supremacy.
Give us foretastes of what will someday fill heaven and earth.
Focus us on Your worthiness as the Son of God.
Fill us with Your resources as the Regent of God.
Fulfill through us Your mission in the purposes of God.
Fire us with Your zeal for the glory of God.
By Your power, transform our lives, our churches, and our cities.
Let Your people here become a showcase of Your majesty before
the nations.
Do all of this in a way that approximates how Your supremacy
will be gloriously manifested when You are fully revealed
at the Consummation of all things! AMEN!

GO DEEPER: Read Acts 1:1-11, 14; 2:1-12, 42-47. Explore chapter 12 and appendix VII at *www.ReadCIA.com*.

TWENTY-THREE

How can God's Word set the stage for a Christ Awakening?

Billy Graham was once asked: "What has been the most exciting part of your ministry? Was it speaking to millions? Being a best-selling author?" The evangelist's instant response was this: "The most satisfying moment in my ministry comes every time I know I have received a word from God and fully delivered it." That should be true for every Messenger of Hope. For this reason Christ proclaimers aim to study and teach God's Word about God's Son for all it is worth!

Of course, every Message of Hope must be personalized, designed in unique ways based on the scope of our own hope in the Master. But for all of us Scripture remains the source of every vision we share. Our fundamental gift to God's people is always the same, God's truth about the supremacy of His Son and the hope in Him this inspires.

> ## QUOTABLE QUOTE
>
> *If we ever tell a particular Bible story without putting it into the overall main Bible story (about Christ), we actually change the meaning of the particular event for us. It becomes a moralistic exhortation to "try harder" rather than a call to live by faith in the work of Christ. There is, in the end, only two ways to read the Bible: Is it basically about me or basically about Jesus?*
>
> (Dr. Tim Keller)

Let's review the key principle: God cannot lead us on the basis of facts we do *not* have. In the same way, the Father cannot lead us into increased hope toward His Son on the basis of an understanding of

His Word about His Son no one is giving us. Equally, we may assume there's *no limit* to how far the Spirit will take us in pursuit of the glory of Christ if we are being filled with a vision for Christ for ALL He is. That's how God's Word sets the stage for a Christ Awakening.

A Simplified Approach

Assume you've been given an opportunity to take a few Christians through a small-group study of a particular Scripture text. As a Messenger of Hope, how would you help them study the Bible in such a way that it becomes a "book of hope" for them? To get you started, here are several approaches that can help you plant in participants a more dynamic biblical vision of the victorious Christ.

Choose a passage that articulates some hope or promise we have in Christ. Possibly start with a portion of Isaiah, Ephesians, Hebrews, or the Gospel of John. Or focus on one of the Messianic Psalms such as Psalm 2; 24; 72; or 110. In any case, ask this set of questions about the text:

1. What promises and prospects are contained in this passage?
2. What will be true of those promises when they reach their ultimate fulfillment in the Consummation to come?
3. What must I see God doing here and now for me to sense that these promises are being fulfilled in more immediate, preliminary ways? What might this look like, in specific terms,

for me? For my church? For my city? For unreached peoples in the world?

4. Whether in ultimate or preliminary forms, how will God's faithfulness to the promises presented in this passage magnify Christ even more?

5. How might any of the previous answers help me know Him better in terms of His supremacy in my life or my world?

6. What immediate steps of obedience do my discoveries require of me?

Using Seven Propositions

To start a second type of study, choose a favorite text. Ask yourself or the group you are leading: How do the promises and prospects in this text expand on one or more of seven key expressions of Christ's supremacy?

1. Is there an insight or promise about who Christ is *to* us? (His nature and His character)

2. Is there an insight or promise about who Christ is *for* us? (From His Incarnation to His crucifixion and Resurrection, to His Ascension, through His intercession, to His return)

3. Is there an insight or promise about who Christ is *over* us? (Head of the Church, Lord of the nations, King of my life)

4. Is there an insight or promise about who Christ is *before* us? (Going ahead of us, opening doors, defeating enemies, leading us in victory)

5. Is there an insight or promise about who Christ is *within* us? (Reproducing His life within us, including His love, holiness, and gifts for ministry)

6. Is there an insight or promise about who Christ is *through* us? (Reaching out to the unreached world through us, either locally or beyond)

7. Is there an insight or promise about who Christ is *upon* us? (As He intensifies and deepens all the other dimensions of His work through the power of the Holy Spirit)

A More Thorough Approach

The following approach may prove the most useful in helping you prepare a Bible study. At the same time it also can turn daily devotional times into powerful encounters with the Lord of glory. Choose only those items that appear most helpful at the moment.

- How does this text, either directly or indirectly, promise that God will manifest to us more of the glory of His Son?

- How does this text speak, directly or indirectly, to the mission thrust of God's people? How might it reinforce for us God's intention to advance Christ's Kingdom by working with His people to lead us into the consummation of all things? How does it point us toward foretastes of that wonderful hope as we serve Christ's global cause right now?

- How does this text, directly or indirectly, highlight God's promise to involve His people in a deeper, healthier, more abundant life in Christ?

- How does this text point us toward the kinds of responses we need to make to Christ as our Lord—for example: How do we need to seek His glory, yield to His call, pursue His agenda, be passionate for His Kingdom, or give Him our heart's devotion and praise? Even more, in what ways does this passage provide disciples with compelling reasons for an all-consuming passion for Christ as our hope?

- Which supporting texts with similar promises might be woven into the prospects offered in this immediate text?

- In what ways might this text give us the right to expect God's intervention in extraordinary ways?

- Does this text reveal any hindrances we must deal with,

whether inside or outside the church, which might prevent a fuller expression of the hope the text offers?

- What does this passage teach us about important steps we should take immediately to prepare, individually or corporately, for greater manifestations of Christ's supremacy among us?

- How do the promises of this passage help us anticipate what we will experience in the Consummation itself? How might this text enlarge and enrich our hope in the supremacy of Christ?

- How would a pursuit of the promises found in this text best express itself practically in our daily discipleship? Be as specific as you can.

- Drawing from this text, what about Christ and His supremacy should we proclaim to our hearers?

- Using the insights from this passage, how would you address any crises of hope or passion that others may be facing right now? With this text in mind, how would you challenge your hearers to reengage with Christ for all He is? What next steps do they need to take to implement renewed commitment to His lordship?

- If the fulfillment of the promises of this text were given fuller expression right now by the power of the Holy Spirit, how might that help make Christ seem more supreme for others?

> ## QUOTABLE QUOTE
>
> *All of us who preach the gospel, I suppose, desire men's conversion. Many, no doubt, are concerned also to glorify God by a faithful declaration of his truth. But how many, when preaching the gospel, are consumed by the longing to magnify Christ—to extol the richness, freedom, and glory of his grace and the perfection of His saving work? The cheap and perfunctory way in which the person of the Savior is sometimes dealt with in modern evangelistic preaching forces this question upon us.... (We must be) concerned above all things to honor Christ: to show his glory to needy men and women ... to recover the over-mastering concern to exalt this mighty Savior.*
>
> (Dr. J. I. Packer)

How might this contribute to curing the crisis of supremacy where you live? Bottom line: What kind of "reforming" of your current perspectives on God's Son should this passage inspire? Where will you begin?

Opening up God's Word to believers in order to impact their vision of Christ and restore their hope in Christ is just one part of our mission as Messengers of Hope—but the most critical part, to be sure.

GO DEEPER: Read Malachi 3:1-4; 16-4:6. Explore chapter 10 and appendix VII at *www.ReadCIA.com*.

TWENTY-FOUR

What if you organize a servant team to foster a Christ Awakening?

By now you're probably asking: How does a Christ Awakening movement begin? How can we go about building a community of hope-filled disciples? How do we get this Campaign of Hope off the ground? How do we find other Messengers of Hope around us? Good news—you can do it! Here are five simple principles many have employed successfully:

1. Uncover Them

A host of potential messengers already reside in our churches. They are a gift from God just as much as the hope within them that so delights them. Many, however, are waiting to be discovered. Or more properly, they need to discover themselves! You could be the key to making this happen.

One way to start is to begin sharing with fellow Christians the larger vision of Christ embodied in this book. Watch for those who light up when you do. Note those who open up to express personal struggles with a spirit of hopelessness they want to conquer. Expect those who have a hunger to experience Christ's power and presence more fully in their lives to say so once they find out you're after the same thing. That's the primary clue that you are in touch with a Messenger of Hope in the making.

2. Define Them

With those who exhibit such initial responses, begin to share more of your own pilgrimage as a Messenger of Hope. In addition, expose to them some of the hundreds of Scriptures related to Christ and Consummation that have touched your heart. Consider taking them through this book in a formal study, investigating some of its central themes. Above all, help them realize how unique their hunger for hope really is and that it is God's gift to them for special purposes.

Invite them to take new steps in their conversion experience, to turn more fully toward Christ and His supremacy. Offer to walk out these changes with them.

3. Gather Them

Introduce them to others with the same passionate hope stirring in their hearts. Bring all your newfound Messengers of Hope together, like coals gathered to start a fire. Set up regular meetings, perhaps in someone's home on a weeknight, or maybe during the Sunday school hour on Sunday morning—again, possibly facilitating weekly discussion sessions to digest this book.

4. Equip Them

Teach them how to expand their vision of Christ and His supremacy, perhaps using one of the approaches to Bible study in chapter 26. Lead them to explore a life of "anticipatory discipleship" (see chapter 13). Provide them with overtly Christ-exalting passages to explore during their daily devotions. Challenge the group to grapple honestly with personal repentance, as needed, to release hope more fully in their lives. Or debrief together the ways some of you may be suffering in your Christian walk. Then explore how the suffering could make God's promises in Christ more alive for you. Of high priority, mentor them in prayer by teaching them how to pray in hope by doing it together (see chapter 27).

> ### QUOTABLE QUOTE
>
> *Father, the hour has come. Glorify your Son now so that he may bring glory to you, for you have given him authority over all men to give eternal life to all that you have given him. And this is eternal life, to know you, the only true God, and him whom you have sent—Jesus Christ.... Father, I want those whom you have given me to be with me where I am; I want them to see that glory which you have made mine—for you loved me before the world began.*
>
> (JOHN 17:1-3, 24 – PHILLIPS TRANSLATION)

5. Release Them

Rally them to join you in spreading their emerging vision of Christ and Consummation among believers right where you live. Encourage them to fulfill their special opportunity to be Messengers of Hope, both in your congregation and beyond. Help them reshape how they proclaim Christ and teach about His supremacy within their families or among their friends. Have them pray over one another as they send one another into the glorious mission of spreading a vision for the supremacy of God's Son.

Blessings a Campaign of Hope Brings to any Church

Focus—As we Christians turn from talking around Christ to start talking about Him, the Lord Jesus will become so much more real for us. We will fulfill Colossians 3:16, as we allow the message about Christ to "dwell in you richly" because together we "teach and admonish one another" with the wisdom that Christ is for us all.

Revitalization—When the majesty, greatness, glory, vastness, and supremacy of God's Son become the overriding themes of our life together, the community will enter into new dimensions of discipleship. We will be blessed by more vibrant worship, stronger prayer gatherings, enriched studies of God's Word, and sharper abilities to see how to love and serve one another.

Obedience—God cannot lead us into a deeper relationship with His Son on the basis of a vision of the supremacy of His Son we fail to give to one another. On the other hand, there are no limits to how far God can take us in our relationship with His Son if we regularly share with one another larger visions of Christ's reign from God's Word.

Christ Awakening Servant Teams

Those truly ready to embrace a Campaign of Hope might agree to serve the movement in a more formal way. This could be a new group or an existing small group in the church that takes on this new mission. One possible name for such a group is a Christ Awakening Servant Team (CAST).

CASTs consist of disciples who have a burning passion to know and live in Jesus for ALL of who He is and then to invite fellow believers to join them in the pursuit of knowing more of His fullness as God's reigning Son. Tactfully and lovingly, CAST members seek to increase the focus among Christians on the glory of Christ. They do this, primarily, by speaking about Him during everyday conversations, especially on Sundays, to help deepen others' love for Jesus as Redeemer and King.

We might say "a CAST serves by casting." It casts a larger vision of God's Son among God's people in the midst of all types of ordinary communications. Quite simply, a CAST ministry comes down to this:

We're connecting Christians more fully to the person of Christ by increasing our conversations about the supremacy of Christ.

Key Characteristics of CASTs

- A CAST ministry is thoroughly biblical. CAST members seek to get more of God's truth about God's Son into regular conversations with God's people. They pass along fresh insights and promises from the multitude of Scriptures about the majesty and supremacy of the Savior. These exchanges allow God's Spirit to connect (or reconnect) believers more fully to the person of the Lord Jesus Christ.

- A CAST ministry is something anyone can take up. In simple and practical ways, CAST members use ordinary opportunities for regular communications—whether one on one or in small-group discussions, in e-mails or phone calls—to remind other disciples of the wonders of who Christ is right now. Any believer seeking to know Christ better and desiring to talk with other believers about fresh discoveries of who He is automatically qualifies for a CAST.

- A CAST has one primary short-range goal: to share God's Word with God's people in such a way that fellow believers walk away from individual conversations or group Bible discussions (or any other times of communication) with (1) a little bit larger vision of Christ, and (2) greater reasons to put their hope in Him.

- A CAST has one primary long-range goal: to multiply themselves through a growing number of believers who follow their example by telling others about the greatness of Christ. A CAST models how all Christians can carry on Christ-focused, Christ-exalting conversations and discussions as a way of life.

- A CAST is pro Christ; it is not anti anything. It's role does not involve critiquing the spiritual vitality of their congregation or its leaders. They minister as servants to the body of Christ. Their desire is to encourage fellow believers toward a more whole-hearted devotion to God's Son for all He is. They do this simply by how they humbly, sensitively weave the truth "in Jesus" (Eph. 4:20-21) into regular conversations.

> **QUOTABLE QUOTE**
>
> *Surely Christ beckons us to repent of hearts that see Him so small that we think our works enrich Him, our programs support Him, our lives are indispensable to His plan. To see Him move and work in power for His name's sake must become our consuming passion, deepening and intensifying as His Spirit takes control of our hearts. Let us settle for nothing less than the explosive inhabitation of the living Lord.*
>
> (TRICIA RHODES)

- A CAST complements the ministry of church leaders. They nurture a "climate of Christ" among church members, which provides many opportunities for believers to open their hearts to a greater devotion to Christ. This is what their leaders long for them to discover. CASTs provide reinforcements to their pastors as they shepherd God's people into fuller dimensions of Christ's reign.

- A CAST works as a team. They support one another in a shared ministry—as they pray for one another, hold one another accountable to their calling, and report to one another the ways they see God connect His children more fully to Christ by increased conversations about Christ. Also, they regularly convene to pray for the seeds they are planting—to pray for a Christ Awakening movement within their congregation and beyond.

First Steps in Forming a CAST

Every step toward forming a CAST should be taken in prayerful consultation with the spiritual leaders of your church. A CAST exists to serve leaders and their people. Please share this chapter with your pastor to help unpack the vision of a CAST and how its ministry can enrich your congregation.

Initially, set up a meeting with several individuals who already demonstrate a growing hunger for the greatness of Christ and who also express longings to see Him receive more fully His rightful adoration in the lives of all believers. This might include people who facilitate or attend prayer groups, guide discipleship groups, or serve as deacons or elders.

In your first session you might want to review, discuss, and pray about ideas presented in this book. Decide where you sense God wants you to go from there. One of the first times you meet, each of you could share with the whole team aspects of your own deepening vision of Christ's majesty. Start connecting one another more fully to the person of Christ by talking with one another about the supremacy of Christ.

Early on, facilitate a session to reflect on portions of God's Word that describe facets of the current reign of God's Son. Every time you meet spend time praying for a Christ Awakening in your own hearts as a CAST, within your congregation, and throughout the church at large.

Your goal is to determine how the Spirit wants your ministry to unfold inside your congregation. Explore some ways to bring more of Christ into your conversations with Christians. Then try your ideas and see what happens. Gather regularly to report what the Spirit is doing with your ongoing conversations with other believers.

Be honest about times you struggle to bring Christ into a conversation and try to figure out why. Brainstorm better ways to sensitively initiate and deepen conversations about Christ. Share stories of evidences of a Christ Awakening you see surfacing within your church.

Keep your spiritual leaders informed of what you are doing and observing. Invite them to rejoice with your CAST in ways you see the Spirit connecting Christians more fully with the person of Christ by increasing their conversations about the supremacy of Christ.

Your Christ Awakening Servant Team can, while serving as Messengers of Hope, colabor with the Spirit to awaken hope more fully for others and thus help empower them to be part of vital advances in the work of Christ.

GO DEEPER: Read Luke 10:1-12, 18-24. Explore chapters 9 and 12 at *www.ReadCIA.com.*

TWENTY-FIVE

Are you ready to be commissioned?

God has a wonderful plan for the nations to reveal the full extent of Christ's supremacy in all things, to all peoples, for all time. He loves His children enough to give each one a significant place in its beginning right now. Every hour the hope of Christ's supremacy should keep us on the cutting edge of His ever-expanding global cause while we serve Him moment by moment as Messengers of Hope.

Christ-Driven Christians

Christ-driven Christians are waiting to arise within any nation, from any race, at any age, out of any denomination. They are first of all Christians—that is, "Christ's ones"—preeminently committed to Christ Himself. He sets the devotion, the direction, and the destiny for their lives, and they know it. These Christians are full of hope, hope in the supremacy of God's Son.

They arise to join in a Campaign of Hope because they realize:

- A deficient vision for Christ's glory plagues today's church.
- A desperate loss of hope in Christ's glory exhausts today's church.
- A pervasive loss of passion toward Christ's glory weakens today's church.
- A diminished worship of Christ's glory impoverishes today's church.

They arise to join in a Campaign of Hope designed to:

- Reawaken God's people to Christ and to the full extent of His supremacy.
- Reawaken God's people to the hope shaped by the glory of Christ's supremacy.
- Redeploy Messengers of Hope who proclaim to God's people the hope found in Christ's supremacy.
- Recapture believers who devote themselves to living in the light of Christ's supremacy.
- Reactivate Christ's servants who prepare themselves to get strategically involved in increased manifestations of Christ's supremacy in churches, communities, and among the nations.

Are you ready to be commissioned as a Messenger of Hope to engage in a Campaign of Hope? If so, from here on out:

- Hope in Christ's supremacy will become the dominating perspective of your life.
- Passion for Christ's supremacy will become the driving motivation of your life.
- A Campaign of Hope will become the decisive ministry of your life as you help fellow Christians recover all the hope and passion that Christ's supremacy is meant to inspire for them.

With humility and gratitude each evening you will say:

I know that this day
my life has counted strategically
for Christ and His Kingdom,
by promoting the hope of His supremacy,
calling my generation to
awake to Christ for ALL He is.

Speaking for myself, I know it's time for me to face straight-on any remaining crises of supremacy in my own life. Each crisis establishes a unique opportunity to grow in Christ.

I affirm: In light of all Christ is, there is far more of Him to know than I've yet discovered. Therefore, I must be passionate to know Him much more than I do. And I must draw near to Him with far more hope in Him than ever before.

I also affirm: God longs for the church to discover much more about His Son. I must, therefore, proclaim Him to Christians more fully than I ever have. Considering the full extent of hope believers share in Christ's supremacy, I must never fear praying for or proclaiming His glory too much.

Facing East

Let me tell you about the Moravians. As a result of a 24-hours-a-day prayer watch for revival and missions, an effort that eventually continued every day for over 100 years(!), these German missionaries circled the globe throughout the 1700s. First, they sent out teams all over Europe to spur Christians toward prayer for a Christ Awakening in their churches. Additionally, at tremendous sacrifice they launched teams to evangelize unreached peoples in Asia, Africa, and North America.

In both endeavors the Moravians labored to reclaim a more comprehensive view of Christ for themselves and others. Hundreds eventually lost their lives for the cause, especially on the mission field. They did so joyfully, however. They were convinced about the triumphs of God's grace yet to come. Their eyes constantly were focused on the supremacy of His Son and the power of His Cross. They inspired subsequent generations to follow in their wake.

In fact, they practiced anticipatory discipleship to such a radical extent it even transformed the way they died! Anywhere they were buried, Moravians asked for their bodies to be laid facing east. They interpreted Scripture to teach that at the Second Coming Jesus would reappear in the eastern sky to bring in the Consummation of the ages.

They were so eager to meet Him that they decided to avoid any need to "turn around" to greet Him when their bodies were raised incorruptible. What magnitude of vision for Christ's supremacy! It propelled one of the greatest Campaigns of Hope of all time.

The Moravians challenge us to examine carefully how we want to position our relationship with the King of kings. Even before Jesus comes back, long before we enter heaven, are we "facing east"?

Ask yourself:

• Do I believe that what I'm doing right now will truly matter when that final hour arrives? In other words, am I facing east?

• Am I committed to developing a greater capacity to know Christ and to enjoy Him forever by the choices I make moment by moment? Am I facing east?

• Am I seeking to live more fully in the power and presence of God's Son, just as I expect to do when I join Him in glory? Am I facing east?

• Am I determined to know and love the Lord of glory in His coronation splendor, not waiting until I die but doing so now with every move I make? Am I facing east?

• Am I willing to help others "face east" with me? Am I willing to labor among God's people, beginning with my own congregation, to call Christians back to a hope and passion that's shaped around the full extent of Christ's supremacy? Will we face east together?

Learning to live "facing east"—experiencing in practical ways what it means to give Christ the supremacy in everything because He is our hope of glory (Col. 1)—is what sustains every Campaign of Hope. It is the key to the cure for the crisis of supremacy. If you agree, then accept your commission!

GO DEEPER: Read 2 Corinthians 4:1-12; 5:14–6:2. Explore chapters 9 and 11 at *www.ReadCIA.com*.

A Personal Word from Richard Ross
My Journey

Condensing the original *CHRIST IS ALL!* from its 470 pages to this book has been one of the most delightful experiences of my life. It has been much like polishing a Stradivarius violin. But that will make sense to you only when you learn about my journey.

I met David Bryant, author of the original work and founder of Proclaim Hope!, at a New York City airport on November 6, 2006. We had just discovered we were on missions that seemed to mesh. Actually, David had been impacting my life for decades before that date.

On October 4, 1997, I stood on the National Mall in Washington, D.C. with well over one million Christian men. The day was called Stand in the Gap. I could not see the stage, but I could hear a voice early in the day that invited us to fall on our faces, silent in prayer before the King of glory. My time with face against the soil was one of the holiest of my life. In 2006 I discovered that the voice calling us to prayer belonged to David Bryant.

For many years I was in Washington, D.C. for the National Day of Prayer. Often my spirit resonated with David Bryant, then chairperson of the National Prayer Committee, as he called Christians throughout America to prayer.

Soon after I met David, I became aware of his seminal book on Christology titled *CHRIST IS ALL! A Joyful Manifesto on the Supremacy of God's Son.* No book I have read in middle adulthood has had a deeper impact on my life. Day by day the Father and the Spirit are waking me up to the glory of the Son.

David has defined the core crisis in the American church. And he has crafted the hope-filled answer to that crisis. He carries the aroma of the Christ who is the focus of his life and message, and I am honored to call him mentor and friend.

Transformation

I have attended church since I was conceived. I began trusting in Christ alone when I was seven. I spent ten years in Christian higher education after high school. I have been a youth pastor, denominational leader, and professor. And yet the Spirit chose to use *CHRIST IS ALL!* to awaken me to several pivotal thoughts, including these:

Who Christ Is—I was completely caught off guard by the fact that who Christ will be on the day of the Second Coming is who He is today. I have always had powerful pictures in my mind about His glorious return, but it had never occurred to me to visualize and approach Him in such regal glory today. That has completely changed the adoration portion of my prayers in the morning and through the day, at least on my good days.

Silence about Christ—To be honest, I was skeptical when David said the church increasingly is not speaking about Christ. So I did what he suggested. I started paying attention. I flipped through best-selling books from Christian publishers and found almost nothing about the current majesty of God's Son. I listened in the halls of conventions and meetings. Again, almost nothing.

Here was the clincher. I observed the national youth convention for an evangelical denomination. Their teenagers filled a domed stadium. For an entire evening I listened for the names of Jesus. Even though some of the finest Christian bands provided the music and the head of the denomination gave the final address, I did not hear one reference to Christ. I can rejoice that God was referenced scores of times in word and song, but that multitude of teenagers did not hear the name of God's Son one time.

Since then I have had that same experience dozens of times around the country. Authors, preachers, and speakers sometimes quote Jesus from His days on earth, but few seek to fill readers or audiences with awe about who our reigning Lord is today.

Now I want to become much more intentional about speaking the name of the Son, about lifting believers' eyes to Him. Most Sunday mornings I preach in different churches in various cities and states. I am asking God to teach me how to preach verse by verse through a passage and, as Spurgeon said, make a beeline for Jesus every time. I am beginning to see God's people embrace an entirely new way of seeing God's Son when the Word clearly is presented in the power of Spirit.

The Coming Generation

The core shortfall of the American church is a crisis of supremacy. That is clear. The next most critical shortfall is perhaps this: the majority of the children of faithful church members fail to walk in faith and stay connected to the church in adulthood. Not only is the church having limited impact on those outside the church; the church cannot even keep its own children in the fold.

Without change the American church will follow the pattern of the churches of Western Europe. The empty churches there will become the empty churches here—not over decades but in one generation.

Now here is a startling thought: The limp faith of Christian teenagers is not because the adult church *has* failed to pass on its faith but because it has passed on its limp faith. In her book *Almost Christian*, Kenda Creasy Dean asks, "What if the blasé religiosity of most American teenagers is not the result of poor communication but the result of excellent communication of a watered-down gospel ...?"

Emerging young adults do not embrace the supremacy of Christ because they have not been around church adults who embrace the supremacy of Christ. Instead, the children of the church have learned to embrace what the adults embrace—the pursuit of personal happiness, comfort, and increasing prosperity. To use the analogy from chapter 1, they are about to marry "the American dream" and only occasionally have a fling with Jesus. Over time they will not even think of Christ at all.

But I am filled with hope rather than gloom. Why? I believe we are seeing the early signs of a spreading Christ Awakening. The very fact that you have been pulled into this book could be an indication something brand-new is happening in you, just as it is in me. And that fresh stirring is happening far and wide.

A Christ Awakening unfolds whenever God's Spirit uses God's Word to reintroduce God's people to God's Son for all He is. A Christ Awakening continues as Christian adults embrace God's Son for all He is and then reveal Him to the next generation in the power of the Spirit. This can happen in three primary ways.

Age-group Ministries—Children's ministers and student ministers newly awakened to Christ can lift the eyes of those they serve to the throne of heaven. Age-group ministers, volunteers, and mentors can be transparent about their own adoration of the Son and the new ways they are arising to join the King in His adventures. At each gathering they can be sure they unfold for the young a larger vision of Christ and His supremacy than they had before they arrived.

The Congregation—Congregations that immerse teenagers in rich webs of relationships have even more influence on the young than youth groups and activities. (Why did we ever think it would be a good idea mostly to isolate youth groups from the church?) If adults value the young and intentionally reach out to build relationships with them, then awakenings among adults will more quickly flood to the next generation.

Families—As valuable as they are, the influence of age-group ministries and congregations pale in comparison to the influence of the home. Awakened parents thrilled with becoming Messengers of Hope need to see their home as their first and most important Campaign of Hope. Christian singles and childless couples also need to pour more of Christ into the next generation, perhaps focusing on nieces, nephews, neighborhood children, and the children of the church.

God has demonstrated in Scripture that He can complete mighty projects in a single day if He chooses. The home may be a tool He will use to accelerate an awakening to His Son—faster than we ever could have imagined. Parents who fall deeply in love with the Lord Christ and are in awe of His majesty will have an almost instant impact on their children and teenagers. Soon we may hear conversations such as these:

Student minister: "Sam, how are things at your house?"

Tenth-grade Sam: "Dude, everything is like, changing, but in a good way. It's hard to put into words. My dad has just gotten a big case of Jesus. My mom, too. You ought to hear our family when we pray now. It's all about Jesus. Nothing is ever going to be the same."

When parents embrace the supremacy of Christ, they will tend to drop the American dream as their dominant religion. Increasingly, their own happiness, comfort, and increasing prosperity will become less important than Christ and His kingdom on earth. And that will even change priorities they have for their children.

How would the teenagers of your church answer the following questions?

My parent would rather see me:
__ Win a full college scholarship.
__ Serve hurting people in the inner city for the sake of Christ.

My parent would rather see me:
__ Introduce three friends to Christ at school.
__ Wear the homecoming queen's crown at halftime.

My parent would rather see me:
__ Lead the team to a state championship.
__ Take the gospel to a village that has never heard of Christ.

It will be a clear sign of awakening when the answers to those questions begin to give top concern to the fame and reign of Christ.

In fact, since 1999 I have been praying for a movement to sweep through our churches. Many long to see every Christian student go to the front lines of missions for a few months in the first year or two after high school. I long to see couples open savings accounts at the birth of babies to fund that future adventure.

If a true Christ Awakening should fuel such a movement, consider what might happen. We might send students to the hard neighborhoods of the U.S. and to all the nations in numbers exceeding those propelled by the Student Volunteer Movement and the Haystack Prayer Meeting. Just think about the implications of that.

Awakening in My Own Family

This is painful to admit. Prior to the beginning of awakening in my life, the American dream had too much sway with me. Every time I changed houses and cars, it was a no-brainer that we would move up to bigger and better. I accepted the common notion that increasing affluence and comfort were simply God's blessings.

Sometimes material blessings are God's intentional gift. When they are, they should be accepted with gratitude and humility. I certainly do not believe self-deprivation is necessary to earn God's favor or to demonstrate holiness.

But awakening is causing my family to see things in new ways. Somehow downsizing and giving away are becoming more exciting than moving "up." Finding new ways to live simply is appealing because it releases new funds to reflect Christ's heart for the poor. Buying smaller rather than bigger opens new ways to speed the gospel to unreached people groups.

If awakening rips through the entire American church, I believe the resulting redirection of resources will alleviate human suffering on a scale world governments could never hope to match. And I believe significant funding immediately will be in place to send believers to every people group on the planet.

One of those going out will be my son. We had to wait 16 years in marriage for the birth of our son, now in college. He is our only living child.

As my wife and I began discussing powerful new insights we were receiving as we read *Christ Is All,* my son immediately became part of the conversation. Only by God's Spirit my son is absolutely alive to Christ these days. Hearing him adore Christ in prayer is holy ground for my wife and me.

Three times we have put him on airplanes for extended service in Third-World countries. Each time we have known the risks. While he is away, we sometimes ask each other, "If he becomes a martyr for Christ in order to establish the church in a new place, are we OK to spend our final decades with no one to care for us and no children or grandchildren at our feet?" We know the deep ache of losing our twins at birth, so we do not answer flippantly. But to see the multiplication of worshippers before the throne for all eternity, we would join the Father who also gave up His only Son.

My Generation

My wife and I want to be just as faithful in going as my son. We have been and want to continue bringing the good news to challenging places.

Awakened adults will direct more of their finances to the nations and to hurting people. That is valuable, but giving cannot take the place of praying deeply and going.

I once took a youth group to serve in an inner-city mission center. Good church people from the suburbs would drive up to donate last year's fashions to the center. Most of them would use the remote button to open the car trunk so we could remove their boxes. They would not even roll down their window for a greeting, lest they catch some urban germ.

But awakened adults will be different as they approach the center. They will think, *Jesus is already inside, loving people and gently helping them reconstruct their lives. I want to get in there and join Him.*

For all who are being awakened to the Son, even retirement will not mean rocking chairs and shuffleboard. It will mean new freedom to take the Campaign of Hope to our Jerusalem, our Judea, and the uttermost parts of the earth.

Let's Join in the Joyful Awakening

Beyond any doubt, you and David and I are off on the grandest adventure of our lives. It is an honor to be walking together and a joy to be walking together toward King Jesus.

As we close this book I think it is entirely appropriate for us to consider these powerful thoughts from David Bryant:

The time has come.

We must spread a vision of the magnificent greatness of Jesus among Christians once again!

The time has come. We must help one another be consumed with His glory as a way of life.

The time has come. We must focus on reforming disciples into strategic bases of operation, men and women who are passionate for the advance of His Kingdom among the nations.

Soon the revelation that *"Christ is all"* will define the greatest answer to the prayers of an entire generation. Soon the proclamation that *"Christ is all"* will resound throughout the church, heard on the lips of all who have reengaged their Savior in the full extent of His supremacy.

Soon Paul's conclusion in Colossians 3:11 that "Christ is all" will become the trademark of those who have recovered all the hope in God we are meant to have.

Yes, "Christ is all."

Surely, among the nations this witness represents the most profound message a human tongue can express.

Surely, within churches so often paralyzed by crises of supremacy, this glorious truth must form the clarion call *from* Christians *to* Christians everywhere.

Surely any Campaign of Hope has no more powerful vision for to spread.

We must aim our campaign
toward those who name the Name,
to reclaim in them the flame
of this radical refrain:

"CHRIST IS ALL!"

Meet David and Richard

David Bryant holds graduate degrees in both biblical studies and missiology from Wheaton (IL) Graduate School and Fuller Theological Seminary. A senior pastor in Ohio for six years and a missions trainer for three years in southern California, he was also minister-at-large with the Madison (WI)-based Inter-Varsity Christian Fellowship for 12 years. In 1988 David founded Concerts of Prayer International and guided it for the next 15 years before launching PROCLAIM HOPE! in 2003. David chaired America's National Prayer Committee for nine years and held leadership roles in a number of national and international coalitions related to prayer, revival, and evangelism. He is the author of best sellers such as *In the Gap* and *With Concerts of Prayer*. *www.ProclaimHope.com*

Richard Ross received a Ph.D. degree in student ministry from Southwestern Seminary in Fort Worth, Texas. He served as a local-church student minister for 30 years. After several part-time positions, he served one church for 12 years and another for 16. Overlapping these roles, Richard served as the youth ministry consultant at LifeWay Christian Resources, the training and publishing agency of  the Southern Baptist Convention. While in that position, Richard cofounded the True Love Waits movement for moral purity among teenagers. Since 2000 Richard has been professor of student ministry at Southwestern Seminary. He is the author or compiler of more than 20 books, including *Student Ministry and the Supremacy of Christ*. *www.RichardARoss.com*

Resources from Proclaim Hope! and Richard Ross

Proclaim Hope! is rooted in **David Bryant's** nearly 20 years serving an unprecedented global prayer movement through his Concerts of Prayer International. Founded in 2001, Proclaim Hope! concentrates on the "fostering and serving of a nationwide Christ Awakening movement." Our mission is: "To awaken throughout the Church fresh hope, passion, prayer, and mission, focused on the Lord Jesus Christ, by proclaiming the full extent of His supremacy and by empowering others to do the same." To that end the ministry offers to individuals and churches a wealth of free written, audio, and video tools. Visit *www.ProclaimHope.org*. and click on the following resources

CHRISTFest

Celebrating the Supremecy
Of God's Glorious Son
For ALL That He Is
With ALL That We Are

Includes:
Program Script
Leader's Manual
Souvenir Bulletin
PowerPoint (350 slides)

PROCLAIM HOPE!

Proclaim Christ's Supremacy * Awaken Hope Fully * Empower the Church

CHRIST ALONE
Eight Encounter Sessions
A study guide for small groups
44 pages / free download

According to **Richard Ross,** the goal of student ministry is students who spend a lifetime embracing the full supremacy of the Son, responding to His majesty in all of life, inviting Christ to live His life through them, and joining Him in making disciples among all peoples. Ross notes, "Student ministry that does not matter for a lifetime does not matter much."

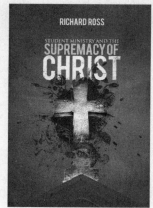

Student Ministry and the Supremacy of Christ proposes a model of student ministry that is far different from the past. This approach calls for:

1. Immersing teenagers in life-on-life, transformational relationships with several godly adults.
2. Drawing teenagers into a web of rich, intergenerational relationships in the congregation.
3. Equipping and supporting parents as those parents take first place in spiritual leadership.

In addition to the core value noted above, the book also offers:

1. Spiritual markers each student should achieve each year of adolescence.
2. A complete plan for assisting students as they make the transition from high school to college/trade school/military.
3. Extensive content church leaders can use as they teach parents how to parent teenagers.
4. A complete strategic planning process for student ministry, including a team-based approach to implementing major student ministry events.

To order, go to *www.crossbooks.com*

For more information about Richard Ross, go to *www.RichardARoss.com*